The Right Sensory Mix

Is It The Right Sensory Mix?

"Diana Derval has written the best book that I have seen on the critical role of the five senses in determining our brand preferences. Her writing is lively, full of relevant case studies, and rich in insights. No marketing department or new product department must proceed without first reading this book."

Philip Kotler, S.C. Johnson & Son Professor of International Marketing,
Kellogg School of Management

"A very innovative and promising approach, which takes into account the physiological diversity of consumers, and proposes to link it with behavioral characteristics; product developers and marketing teams should read this book in order to take advantage of the variability of sensory perceptions."

Nathalie Jacquet, Head of Sensory Analysis & New Products Development,
Research Center Pernod Ricard

"Five golden stars! "The Right Sensory Mix" takes the concepts of genetics and neuroendocrinology and applies them to predict consumer behavior. The text is intellectually brilliant and delightful. Read the book and you will want to adapt Prof. Derval's model because the book discloses in detail how sensory networks and the Hormonal Quotient^{TM} (HQ) help predict consumer's attitudes and behavior, the data obtained from her own scientific approach, to how actually the technique works as exemplified by well known commercial brands. Therefore, I highly recommend the "The Right Sensory Mix" for all, students, professionals and scientists who don't want to be left behind."

Magda Carvalho, PhD Genetics, Faculty Member as Instructor in Medicine at Cornell Medical School
(New York), J.D., US Patent Attorney

"Diana Derval invites us to explore our senses, with the help of fascinating scientific discoveries – and a great sense of humor. Reading her book was like an eye-opener: it changed my vision of marketing and made me consider a new consumer approach."

Alexis Mühlhoff, Head of Marketing, Komatsu

"Professor Diana Derval is inspiring you, with mental agility, always seizing any opportunity to break 'conventional' consumer research/insights with a new, creative, scientific approach, resulting in unexpected ways to predict consumer behaviors and new ways of identifying unexplored, profitable market segments. A fascinating book!"

Markus Kohler, Director Packaging at Philip Morris International

"Thanks to her discovery concerning the relationship between hormones and sensory sensitivity, Diana Derval proposes an amazing scientific approach to accurately profile consumers, according to their Hormonal Quotient^{TM} (HQ). She succeeds in explaining her findings on smell, color, and texture preferences in a very simple and lively way making her book so pleasant to read. This original tool can be recommended for marketing profiling or in addition to a psychology study to comprehend one's personality."

Wai Wong, accessory group development manager, Sephora/LVMH Group.

"Great book for understanding consumer sensory behavior."

L'Oréal Benelux

"Professor Diana Derval excels in building a bridge between scientific research and business applications. She shares the latest scientific insights on sensory perception and human behavior in a clear and accessible way. Illustrated by many business cases analyzed with humor, the book conveys a brilliant train of thought that sticks to the brain."

Mark van Hagen, Senior Project Leader Strategic Research, NS (Dutch Railways)

Diana Derval

The Right Sensory Mix

Targeting Consumer Product Development
Scientifically

 Springer

Diana Derval
DervalResearch
Keizersgracht 44F
1015 CR Amsterdam
The Netherlands
e-mail: diana.derval@derval-research.com
website: http://www.derval-research.com

ISBN 978-3-642-12092-3   e-ISBN 978-3-642-12093-0

DOI 10.1007/978-3-642-12093-0

Springer Heidelberg Dordrecht London New York

Library of Congress Control Number: 2010933483

© Springer-Verlag Berlin Heidelberg 2010

Cover design: WMXDesign GmbH

Printed on acid-free paper

Springer is part of Springer Science+Business Media (www.springer.com)

To Johan, my carousel of love

Foreword

Since Aristotle we are familiar with the traditional five senses: sight, hearing, touch, smell and taste. But to what extent do we actually understand them? As Diana Derval shows in her remarkable guide through the secrets of human perception, we are only getting started in understanding how our senses function. And what a wonderful journey it is to explore perception beyond the frontiers we grew up with. Will we ever get there? Will we ever understand the nature of our senses, or even get to an agreement on, let's say, taste? Of course not. Never! As Friedrich Nietzsche wrote in *Thus Spoke Zarathustra* "All life is a dispute about taste and tasting! Taste: that is weight at the same time, and scales and weigher; and alas for every living thing that would live without dispute about weight and scales and weigher!"

To some, this notion of an eternal quest might feel uncomfortable. For us at Sofitel Amsterdam The Grand, the seemingly endless variety of senses offers a fantastic world of excitement and opportunity we travel through day and night. In the atmosphere of pleasure, magic, and comfort we create at our place, understanding sensory perception is the fundamental key to our success in exceeding the expectation of our guests. Delivering the Right Sensory Mix is what we strive for continuously—a passion we share with Prof. Derval.

Bon Appetit!

Robert-Jan Woltering
General Manager
Sofitel Amsterdam The Grand

Acknowledgments

I would like to thank the business, marketing, product development, and R&D professionals who contributed to this book.

Special thanks to Samy Liechti, CEO of Backsocks.com, Rocky Af Ekenstam Brennicke, Marketing Director at Björn Borg, Brigit Mettra, CEO of La Favorite, for sharing their success stories.

Un grand merci to Robert-Jan Woltering, General Manager of the *Sofitel Amsterdam The Grand*, for sharing his passion for human sensory perception, and writing the foreword to this book. Thanks to Nynke M. van der Berg, Marketing Manager, for her contribution

Vielen dank to Frank Fleck, VP Corporate Marketing at *Carl Zeiss Vision*, to Boris Dejonckheere, Marketing Director Europe, for the fascinating research on hormones and vision conducted together with Herbert Krug R&D teams and lead optician Frits Blij, from De Kijkkamer.

I am very grateful to Michael and Charles McGinley, Managers of *St. Croix Sensory Inc.*, for their great support and expertise on smell perception, and for lending us a Nasal Ranger.

Hartelijk dank to Mark van Hagen, Researcher at the *Dutch Railways (NS)*, Jessica Sauren, Ad Pruyn, and Mirjam Galetzka, from the University of Twente, for the fantastic observations and measurements done together on thousands of train travelers.

A big thank you to Rie Søbye, Marketing Manager at Interacoustics, for providing us with a clinical OtoAcoustic Emissions Reader. Thanks to Daniel Flück, Colblindor, for granting permission to use the color vision test and to Prof. Kitaoka for the amazing turtle illusion.

A hug for Emmanuelle Sangouard, who agreed to share her incredible expertise in beauty care products.

A warm thank you to all the subjects who participated in our research and experiments, and in particular the ARC rugby team, my students in innovation, entrepreneurship, and sensory science at ESSEC Paris-Singapore Business School, my MBA students in health communications at University Pole Leonard de Vinci, and my executive MBA students from the Robert Kennedy College/University of Wales.

A big thank you to my colleagues, professors and researchers from ESSEC Paris-Singapore Business School, Robert Kennedy College, University of Wales, University Pole Leonard de Vinci, International School of Management, Fudan University in Shanghai, the Society for Behavioral Neuroendocrinology, the Society for Sensory Professionals, the Market Research Society, MOA, and ESOMAR, for their support.

Many thanks to all the scientists, sensory professionals, and researchers whose work inspired my research, with a special mention for John T. Manning, on hormones and behavior, Linda Bartoshuk on taste perception, Martin Robinette on otoacoustic emissions, Martin Bronwen on metabolism and taste and smell perception, Kimberly Jameson on color perception.

I am grateful to DervalResearch clients, teams, partners, and shareholders for their support. Special thanks to Patricia Schneiders, Director of the French Chamber of Commerce in the Netherlands, Pierre Winkel, Director at Natexis, and Sandrine Goldie, for their encouragements, to Natalie Ardet for her contribution on innovation and sustainability, to Marja Salaspuro for her availability and research work, and Vlad Kolarov for the awesome illustrations.

Great thanks to David Gardner, Pacific Consultants Group, Inge Kaaijk-Wijdogen, L'Oréal, Nathalie Jacquet, Pernod Ricard, Herbert Krug, Carl Zeiss Vision, Markus Kohler, Philip Morris, Francois-Xavier Albouy, LEGO, and Iolanda Meehan Niculescu, Philips, for their review, and constructive feedback.

Dankjewel to my dear friends Esperance, Cecilia, Nicolas, Lizet, Anna, Susan, Jean-Christophe, and to my friends at EPWN, VMC, CFCI, Club Affaires, Marcus Evans, Luxe Pack, and WTG Events.

I thank from the bottom of my heart Barbara Fess, my editor at Springer for her trust and guidelines.

Trillions of thank yous go to Johan, who supported me during my research, provided me with lots of love and coffee, and helped me design and patent an awesome Hormonal Quotient^{TM} (HQ) Calculator.

I would also like to thank you, dear reader.

Contents

Chapter 1
Coming to Our Senses

"Research is to see what everybody else has seen, and to think what nobody else
has thought"

Albert Szent-Györgyi, Hungarian Biochemist,
1937 Nobel Prize for Medicine (1893–1986)

Recent breakthroughs in human sensory perception and neurosciences offer endless opportunities in the field of product development. The first chapter shows how to easily generate groundbreaking insights with a more scientific approach. The critical role of consumers' senses is analyzed through the study of *Coke Zero* and *Red Bull*, and the secrets of taste are revealed.

1.1 Introduction

In this chapter, we come to our senses and start by answering the following critical questions in Sect. 1.2 with the coffee case (Fig. 1.1):

- Why do customers prefer a product?
- Which customers would like my product and why?
- How can I attract more of these customers?
- What is the role of culture, brand credibility and emotions on the purchasing decision?

Our investigations lead us into the fascinating world of sensory perception and we discover in Sect. 1.3 why consumer insights are on the tip of our tongue, how taste works, and the possible business applications.

In Sect. 1.4, we see how sensory receptors, body, and brain cooperate to respond to external stimuli and how we can use this knowledge in product development.

We see how to generate groundbreaking insights in Sect. 1.5, and use frameworks like personas and the innovation path matrix to identify relevant innovations.

Major take-aways are provided in Sect. 1.6.

D. Derval, *The Right Sensory Mix*, DOI: 10.1007/978-3-642-12093-0_1,
© Springer-Verlag Berlin Heidelberg 2010

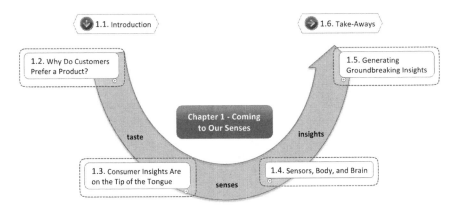

Fig. 1.1 Content of Chap. 1

1.2 Why Do Customers Prefer a Product? The Coffee Case

My sensory journey started around a cup of coffee—a business related one. It was our very first challenging mission: *"Why do consumers prefer a certain type of coffee? Is it for cultural reasons—they prepare it in a certain way in their country—or because of the brand—that is well known—or because the product triggers certain emotions—reminding them of their grand'ma preparing coffee?"* Good question indeed: Why do some consumers prefer a strong espresso and others a watery coffee? By the way, why do some add sugar and others milk? Wait a minute—first of all, why do some consumers drink tea?

The answer we came up with was at the same time totally unexpected and so obvious: it is the taste.

I will show you through this real coffee case how sensory perception, often underestimated, can make or break a product.

1.2.1 The Cultural Myth

The first objection we faced was: *"Taste has nothing to do with this, Italians have been drinking espresso and Swedes watery coffee for generations. It is just cultural!"* It is true that specific consumption patterns can be observed locally. The point is, do Swedes drink watery coffee because their parents and grand parents did? Or do Swedes like watery coffee and their parents and grand parents happened to like it too, the same for their compatriots, and that is the reason why it became the local standard?

We have a nice example of mutation in cultural standards in the Netherlands. The Dutch love coffee and traditionally drink a stronger variety of beans, robusta, because their explorers brought it back from Africa. More than two-third of the population puts milk in the coffee because otherwise it is a bit too strong. When they had the opportunity to taste a milder coffee, from arabica beans, they naturally switched to it as it fits better their taste.

I therefore see culture as a temporary local standard that can evolve if better options are proposed, instead of an immutable tradition.

1.2.2 Brand Legitimacy

The second objection we faced was: "*Anyway, sales are less than expected in some countries because our brand is not very well known in this product category*". A noted example of this phenomenon is Bic, successful colorful writing pens manufacturer, who made a total flop when launching a perfume. Apparently people were not making a positive association with cheap plastic pens and fragrance.

What about new players? Companies like Red Bull, who experienced an overnight success. They did not have any brand legitimacy. Or maybe not being known at all is better than being known for something else?

An intriguing example is then the Michelin case. I had a chance to work for the Michelin man, not with their tires, but their maps and Red Guide. I was amazed to learn that the Clermont-Ferrand firm had the idea to design and print maps and guides to encourage drivers to use their tires—genius! So you have an industrial company, famous worldwide for its black and smelly rubber tires, becoming also a first-class leading food critic with the Michelin Red Guide. Intriguing, no?

I decided to check this coffee story in one of the concerned countries, Germany. I went to the supermarket, bought the leading local coffee brand and tasted it. Aha, it was less bitter and more sour. In fact, the local brand was more legitimate—not because it had been in the market for a longer time, but because it actually understood better the consumers' expectations in terms of taste.

1.2.3 Triggering Emotions

The third objection we faced was: "*In the end, what matters is triggering emotions in consumers' mind. They will then associate the brand positively and not even think of the product's intrinsic properties*". Maybe this fascination for emotions comes from the fact that we still have a lot to learn in this field. Whether they are adaptive or innate, we consider emotions as negative, positive, or neutral for us.

An *adaptive* emotion could be, last time grandma did a coffee we spent a nice day together. As soon as I smell the coffee, I remember that day and feel good. An *innate* emotion would be closer to an instinctive response, like for instance disgust or pleasure. Maybe there is just a positive impact of coffee smell on my sensors and each time I smell coffee it happens again?

Did You Know? Disgust has a Face

The most effective method to properly identify emotions is facial recognition. Innate emotions like anger, contempt, disgust, fear, happiness, joy, sadness, and surprise are expressed by the same facial expressions worldwide. Recent research demonstrated that blind and non-blind judoka present the exact same sad face in case of defeat with a mouth corner depressed, and inner corner eyebrows raised.

Good to know for your next tasting panels, disgust is expressed by the following facial expression: lower lip turned down, upper lip raised, expiration, mouth open, spitting, blowing out, protruding lips, clearing throat sound, lower lip, tongue protruded (Matsumoto 2009)!

1.2.4 The Market Response

The decision was reached to launch a new mainstream coffee product in Europe. The blend was first tasted internally, at headquarters, by the sales and marketing team. Out of the 10 team members, nine thought the coffee was perfect and one reported that the taste was a bit too bitter. To make things right, tasting panels were organized with a representative mix of 200 consumers, both men and women. The outcome was less unanimous but a good half of the panelists were very positive about this new coffee. The sales and marketing teams were confident, as they also liked the taste, and the product hit the market.

The response of the consumers was quasi-unanimous and could be summarized in one word, or one face, 'disgusting'. How come?

The answer was just here, on the tip of our tongue.

1.3 Consumer Insights Are on the Tip of the Tongue

Why did Red Bull become an overnight success in spite of the terrible feedback from the first consumers' tasting panels? Why is Red Bull now sponsoring extreme sports? Why should The Coca-Cola Company stop wasting colossal advertising budget on men's target for its Coke Zero? The answers to these questions and many more are here, on the tip of our tongue! Let us discover the arcanes of taste. We will have a closer look at why tasting panels can be unreliable. This will help us solve our coffee mystery.

1.3.1 The Secrets of Taste Perception

When observing eating and drinking habits—think of club-goers drinking Red Bull or people tasting a difference between Diet Coke and Coke Zero—we may wonder whether we all share the same perception of taste.

Fig. 1.2 Taste buds (printed
with DervalResearch
permission)

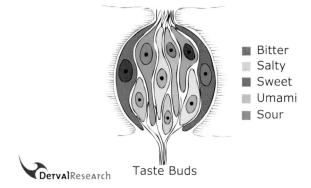

- Bitter
- Salty
- Sweet
- Umami
- Sour

Taste Buds

1.3.1.1 Taste Buds

Depending on our gender, ethnicity and age, the number of taste buds we host on
our tongue can vary between 11 and 1,100/cm^2 (Fig. 1.2).

Each taste bud helps to perceive bitter, sweet, salt, sour, and umami (umami
corresponds to the glutamate taste present in meat, cheese, and mushrooms).

1.3.1.2 Taste Profiles

Based on the number of taste buds, people can be classified into three categories
(Fig. 1.3):

- Super-tasters: super-tasters are very sensitive to alcohol, strong coffee, bitter
  vegetables, too-fat and too-sweet meals. They perceive sugar as twice as sweet.
  Not the best target for Red Bull!
- Medium-tasters: medium-tasters are more easy going but still prefer sweet to
  bitter food. They perceive aspartame with a bitter after-taste. So they will
  definitively prefer a Coke Zero to a Diet Coke.
- Non-tasters: non-tasters can eat and drink almost anything.
  In Europe, 25% of the population can be considered as non-taster, 50% as
  medium-taster and 25% as super-taster.

Fig. 1.3 Taste profiles
(printed with DervalResearch
permission)

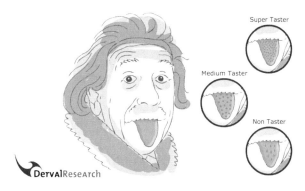

Super Taster

Medium Taster

Non Taster

Taste profile identification can be done by having people taste a strip of phenylthiocarbamide (PTC), an organic compound. Super-tasters will perceive the strip as very bitter, medium-tasters as bitter, whereas non-tasters will perceive it as being just a strip of paper (Table 1.1).

You can check your sensory profile on http://www.derval-research.com

1.3.1.3 Taste Modifiers

Women are more likely to be tasters than men. They are particularly sensitive when pregnant or during menstruation. The taste perception decreases also with age (Fig. 1.4).

The variation in the taste perception between males and females, younger and older, Caucasian and Asian is due to the influence of hormones, as we will see in Chap. 3.

Factors such as our mood and the temperature can also enhance perceived taste. A warm beer or a cold coffee will for instance taste more bitter.

1.3.2 Tasting Panels

Back to our coffee mystery! We thought it might be interesting to check the representativeness of the panel, but not in terms of gender, or age: in terms of taste. We measured the sensitivity to bitterness, of the different groups involved, with PTC strips and here are the surprising results:

- Sales and marketing teams: among the 300 employees, men and women, from the 25 sales and marketing departments worldwide, only 20% perceived the bitter taste. So 80% of the sales and marketing teams from the firm were non-tasters (Table 1.2).
- Tasting panels: the PTC test conducted on the 200 panelists helped determine that 54% of the women and 51% of the men were non-tasters.
- Market: non-tasters represent only 25% of the European population (Bartoshuk 1994).

In the end, there were two times more non-tasters among the panelists, and three times more non-tasters among the sales and marketing teams than among the target population. That is not exactly representative. This experiment was a real eye-opener for many marketing and product development professionals because it showed that individuals have a different perception of the same stimulus, teams developing products are not necessarily representative of their target customers, and science can help make reliable business decisions.

Let us have a look at what happens when you know your target customer (or not?) with the Red Bull and the Coke Zero cases.

Table 1.1 Taste perception (Bartoshuk 1994)

	Non-tasters	Medium-tasters	Super-tasters
Bitter	Perceives saccharin as sweet	Perceives saccharin with a bitter after-taste	Perceives saccharin as very bitter Dislikes bitter vegetables like cabbage, spinach, broccoli, cauliflower or eats them with sauce containing cheese, cream, or butter Dislikes coffee/espresso or drinks it with milk and sugar
Sweet	Perceives sugar as sweet Female non-tasters love sweets	Perceives sugar as sweet Likes better sweet than bitter tasting food and beverages	Perceives sugar as twice as sweet Likes better sweet than bitter tasting food and beverages Like sweets 'so-so'
Spicy	Can eat spicy food	Can eat spicy food	Chili and black pepper are irritating
Alcohol	Perceived as sweet rather than bitter	Can drink alcohol	Alcohol is irritating
Fat	Can eat fatty food	Can eat fatty food	Hypersensitive to fat, perceived as a 'touch' and not a taste
Taste buds	Seed-shaped, in a limited number	Round shaped, in a fair number	Tongue covered with taste buds
PTC test	Paper taste	Bitter taste	Very bitter taste
Segment	25% of the population, mainly men	50% of the population	25% of the population, mainly women

Fig. 1.4 Taste modifiers
(printed with DervalResearch
permission)

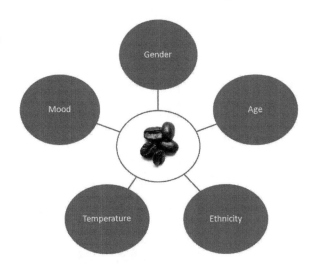

1.3.3 Red Bull, the Extreme Taste

How did Red Bull become the leading energy drink, selling billions of cans
worldwide every year?

The smart marketing strategy contributed, certainly. The Austrian firm targeted
consumers looking for a handy energy shot: drivers, club-goers, and sports people.
By making the functional drink available on the road, in dance and sports clubs—
usually by providing the fridge—Red Bull developed a powerful distribution and
word-of-mouth strategy.

But what about the taste? Was it not reviewed a 'D' by BevNet.com and judged
as 'disgusting' by the tasting panel? True. The point is that the consumers find the
Haribo-gold-bears-candy-taste perfectly fine (Wipperfurth 2005). Probably
another wrong panel recruitment.

Observing that the best fit was with people involved with extreme sports, the
firm led by CEO Dietrich Mateschitz, now devotes most of its sales and marketing
budget sponsoring motor, aerial, and adventure sports. In 2009, Red Bull is official
sponsor of the X-Fighters, a freestyle motocross event, with a budget of 5 million
dollars. The expected gains are high as the brand sold 36 million cans during the
2008 Red Bull Air Race (Robyn 2009). For some reason—that will be revealed in
Chap. 3—extreme sports players have fewer taste buds than average consumers.
Therefore, the very sweet taste of Red Bull is perfectly fine for them.

Table 1.2 Taste profile per group involved (Derval 2009a, b)

	N	Non-taster (%)	Taster (%)
Sales and marketing managers	300	80	20
Tasting panel	200	53	47
Market		25	75

1.3.4 *The* Coke Zero *Paradox*

Neville Isdell, CEO of The Coca-Cola Company from 2004 to 2008, decided to launch a new major product: Coca-Cola Zero. At last, after 22 years of little to no innovation, the Atlanta firm decided to revolutionize the market with a sugar-free Coke for men. The whole marketing mix is very consistent and men-oriented: the packaging is black and sober, the website promotes racing, and the advertising spots feature explosions and sexy girls. The colossal advertising budget, already 76 million dollar for the launch in 2006, did not really help convert as many males as planned. Scott Williamson, Coca Cola spokesperson, admitted 2 years after the launch that Zero was equally consumed by men and women (Howard 2007).

Is the Coca-Cola Zero marketing campaign with half-naked women pole-dancing appealing to women? Probably not. But the taste surely is! Let us have a closer look at the brand's diet drinks: Diet Coke is sweetened mainly with aspartame—a sweetener that has a bitter after-taste—and since recently a bit of acesulfame potassium whereas Zero contains an equal mix between aspartame and acesulfame potassium (Feldman 2008). Women happen to be, on average, more sensitive to bitterness than men. So women who tried Coke Zero in spite of the men-targeted campaign naturally abandoned Diet Coke to switch to Zero. It is difficult to evaluate the sales loss due to the wrong targeting, but we can guess that Zero will soon be re-positioned as the official Diet Coke, for men and women. Or more specifically, for consumers with many taste buds and who are weight-conscious.

In tasting, as you can see from the Red Bull, Coke Zero, and the Coffee Case, there is no universal good taste, and the key is 'Who' is tasting.

1.3.5 *Why Rugby Men Should Date Nurses*

Many publications confirm that women are, on average, more sensitive to taste than men. For instance, research conducted on 187 women and 87 men of various ages (Michon et al. 2009), demonstrated that women are more able to perceive bitter and sour taste.

Further measurements conducted on 102 Caucasian women in their 30s, with various vocations, like entrepreneurs, housewives, and nurses, show huge differences in perception of taste among women (Derval 2009a, b). All tested women entrepreneurs were super-tasters and all nurses non-tasters. Maybe that is why complaints on hospital food are never taken seriously?

I had the privilege to measure the taste perception of members of a rugby team—many thanks to the ARC 1890 rugby club!—and it seems like their taste buds are not very numerous. The good news is that the beer tastes sweet after the matches. We will see in Chap. 3 why groups of people with the same vocation and hobbies have also a similar sensory perception.

In the meantime, nurses would be the perfect date for rugby men: they could heal their wounds and would both pay more attention to the ambience and conversation than to the food.

1.3.6 Taste Profiles: Business Applications

Adapting product or services to consumers' taste offers great opportunities on the market. I selected for you the following business applications, just to give you an idea of the realm of possibilities.

No. 1   Proposing special meals for super-tasters in schools, planes, and hotels.
No. 2   Adapting drugs tastes and textures (syrup, pills) to each taste profile.
No. 3   Creating an "approved by super-tasters" label to help non-tasters buy healthy food—in spite of the fact that they cannot taste the difference.
No. 4   Offering super-tasters, medium-tasters, and non-taster cook-books with targeted recipes.
No. 5   Designing party beverages and snacks with less sugar, fat, salt, and alcohol suited for medium and super-tasters.

Sensory perception can explain many consumers' reactions in the market. But how do our body, brain, and senses work together?

1.4 Sensors, Body, and Brain

Throughout the day we are bombarded by signals requiring a specific answer or action. Imagine a small child: "I am hungry!", "Why do we have to walk?", "Why is it dark at night?" Our body, sensors, and brain team up to deliver a response to each of these requests. Let us see how it works and how this knowledge can help us develop relevant products.

1.4.1 Senses, and Millions of Sensors

In the same way our tongue is covered with taste buds, our body is covered with millions of sensors, comprising our nervous system (Table 1.3).

Sensors detect different types of stimuli, like pressure, temperature change, or chemicals. Nocireceptors are not a species of dinosaur, but just our pain sensors. As we will see throughout the different chapters, excessive stimuli, even if related to smell or taste are in fact detected and managed by dedicated pain sensors.

Commonly known senses are smell, taste, vision, hearing, and touch. Other senses are balance (located in the ear), temperature, pain, and proprioception—our ability to locate our nose wherever we are!

Table 1.3 Type of sensors (Marieb 2007)

Type of sensors	Detected stimuli	Location
Mechanoreceptors	Touch, vibration, stretch, movement, hearing, vision	Skin, hair follicles, genitalia, fingertips, feet sole, eyelids, muscles, head
Thermoreceptors	Temperature change	Skin
Chemoreceptors	Smell, taste, chemicals	Body tissues, head
Nocireceptors	Excessive pressure, temperature, smell, or taste	Body tissues

Proprioception is the awareness of our positioning and movements. We can draw a parallel between proprioception and the 'dead reckoning' function of a GPS navigation device (it is a former TomTom R&D manager speaking!). When you enter a tunnel, the device does not receive the positioning by satellite anymore. It relies then on the sensors of the car: the accelerometer, that indicates the velocity, and the gyroscope, that shows the orientation. Dancers and rugby men for instance are equipped with cutting-edge biological navigation devices.

1.4.2 Stimulus and Response

Information received by sensors is a sensation. Once interpreted by our brain, it becomes a perception (Marieb 2007). Our body then gives an appropriate (or not!) response. All of these responses have an impact on our balance and immune system. I will share specific examples in the next chapter. The facial expressions mentioned earlier for instance are shaped by the nerves and muscles of our face in a fast decision-making process: an innate response (Fig. 1.5).

A lot of attention is given to the brain, which is considered as a central point of decision. However the question is how far is the brain involved in the discussion between our sensors?

Fig. 1.5 Sensor response monitoring (printed with DervalResearch permission)

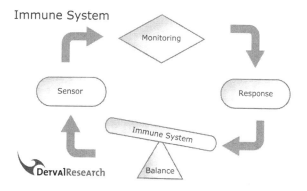

1.4.3 Who's the Boss?

Our brain hosts our core nervous system in the cerebral cortex. Located on the top of the brain, the cerebral cortex includes the following areas related to sensors (Marieb 2007):

- A *spatial discrimination area*, that manages the input from the skin and the proprioception receptors.
- A *somatosensory association area*, that analyzes all the sensory inputs to guess what object is being sensed.
- A *visual area*, that analyzes color, form, and movement.
- An *auditory area*, that processes and stores sound.
- An *olfactory area*, that manages some aspects of smell.
- A *gustatory area*, perceiving taste.
- A *visceral area*, managing input from stomach, lungs, and bladder (exactly, that is the one telling you it is time to go to the toilets!).
- A *vestibular area*, managing balance.

The brain manages all these sensory inputs and prevents us from an overload, thanks to its selective attention. The *cocktail-party phenomenon* illustrates this ability we have to focus: during a party, provided the people we talk to are interesting, we tend to not hear the other conversations around. Except when our name is pronounced, then suddenly, we hear them. Our brain was in fact filtering all the surrounding stimuli (Pinel 2007).

That being said, if you do not sense a stimulus, there is nothing to process, manage, interpret, or store, in the brain. So before wondering how, when, and why consumers are basing decisions on stimuli we send them through our products, it is wise to check if they actually sense those stimuli.

1.4.4 Sensory Science and Product Development

Many factors can influence consumers' decisions, like for instance their mood, the external temperature, or the color of the socks of the cashier. In order to develop products in an effective way, we benefit from checking those factors in a certain order. You know a bit like the IT helpdesk does, in the TV serie *The IT Crowd* (Linehan 2006), when people call in about their dysfunctioning PC:

1. "Have you tried turning off and on again?"
2. "Have you made sure it is plugged in?"

Translated into sensory science, it would be:

1. "Did you try to resend your stimulus?"
2. "Does the consumer sense the stimulus at all?"

In the coffee case, it is useful and easy to check the consumer's perception of bitterness before going further into culture, brand, and emotion aspects. The role of sensory science is therefore becoming more strategic. Firms are now analyzing their products in a very systematic way, using sensory maps and other statistical tools. What has been less investigated so far, however, is analyzing the target customers. Identifying the personas, and their sensory perception, as we will see right now, is the best way to generate groundbreaking insights.

1.5 Generating Groundbreaking Insights

The challenge when generating insights is to be at the same time creative and relevant. Most methods used lead to an abundance of far-fetched projects and then to a short-list of reasonable products nobody needs. We will see how to use powerful reasoning techniques, observe target customers, brainstorm in a constructive way, having customers in mind, and get inspired from other industries serving them.

1.5.1 Deduction, Induction, and Retroduction

The tricky part is how to generate, or at least identify, a great idea? Charles Sanders Peirce, scientist, philosopher, and founder of pragmatism, introduced in 1865 a way of thinking logically called retroduction, or abduction (Peirce 1992).

Whereas deduction and induction process only the links between information that are known, retroduction introduces in the reasoning, while building a model, a creative insight with a hypothesis to be verified. The model can in this way even be applied to cases that were not observed.

Here is how it works:

- Deduction: (a) she is not married → (b) that is why she does not wear a wedding ring.
- Induction: (b) she does not wear any wedding ring → (a) she must be single.
- Retroduction: she does not wear any wedding ring → (hypothesis by induction) h1. she might be divorced → (deduction) that is why she does not wear a wedding ring.

This typical Sherlock Holmes reasoning, can get you into trouble. I refer here to the moment in the movie where our detective realizes that the lady is actually not divorced but a widow (Ritchie 2009). On the other hand, retroduction can earn you groundbreaking innovations if your hypothesis is validated. Current applications of retroduction can be found in the field of sociological prediction, pharmacological discoveries, artificial intelligence, and industrial production processes. As algorithms based on retroduction are similar to those used for findings subgraphs or arbitrary graphs, this way of reasoning is now critical in "social network analysis", to hunt down organized crime and terrorism (Stanford 2009).

Analogy is often used to find relevant hypotheses. What happened in similar cases, what was the explanation of a certain behavior we observed? If this approach might appear as 'intuitive' to sequential minds, it is in fact scientific as it proceeds from making observations, and building and validating hypotheses.

If we go back to our coffee case, it would be something like:

- Deduction: (a) he likes strong coffee → (b) that is why he drinks espresso.
- Induction: (b) he drinks espresso → (a) he must like strong coffee.
- Retroduction: (observation) he drinks espresso → (hypothesis by induction) he might be less sensitive to bitterness → (deduction) that is why he likes strong coffee → (validation) indeed, he does not taste the bitterness of the PTC strip—Elementary, Dr. Watson!

The key is therefore to observe consumers and to try to build a model that will help come up with groundbreaking insights.

1.5.2 Observing Personas versus Asking

Firms need to know more about their customers to generate relevant and groundbreaking insights. The first step is to clarify the target groups. Easier to say than to do? Right, many corporate segmentations are as vague as:

- Women between 20 and 65 years old.
- 52% have children.
- 54% have an average income.

Socio-demographic and statistical data—often meaningless if not contradictory—lead to poor or no segmentation at all. As a result, firms develop 'one-size-fits-all' products with the risk to miss their target customers and to pave the way for competition. It is more constructive to focus instead on people's motivation, state of mind, usages, and of course perception. Some critical questions must be answered before designing a product or service. Back in 1973, Peter Drucker already found out that: "the aim of marketing is to know and understand the customer so well that the product or service fits him and sells itself." And the best way to do so, is to observe consumers rather than to ask them.

Here's an example: When the new Michelin website with route planning and hotel and restaurant information went live, the number of visitors quickly broke through 15 million per month—an achievement at European level!—and we had to have a look at our server capacity to make sure it could cope with this heavy traffic. We saw that the vast majority of the users were planning their weekend on Monday morning, probably desperate to come back to work. When asking around which day of the week people plan their week-end, the answer we got was Thursday or Friday. People are not necessarily telling lies, it is just that they did not pay attention and when they think of it, the end of the week sounds more logical. So instead of asking consumers their expressed needs and then trying to guess their hidden needs, let us just observe them and debrief with them afterwards on why they acted in a certain way.

Tammo de Ligny, Senior Director of Design at Philips Consumer Lifestyle, confirmed to me that understanding trends is at Philips more based on observations than on surveys (Derval 2009a, b). The objective is to answer questions like "What do users need and want when they wake up in the morning?" Product design uses a *personas* database that includes the users' education, insights, and income. He recalled Henry Ford's quote "If I had asked my customers what they wanted, they would have said a faster horse". This method is shared by all departments within the company, which allows a consistent and global approach based on the con- sumers' profile and needs. Leading brands use the *Persona* framework for a consistent and targeted approach of their customers based on their profile and expectations.

Here is an easy method to identify your own *personas* in three steps (Derval 2009a, b): build a vision, then describe, and validate the personas.

1.5.2.1 Step 1: Build a Vision

What are the differences between your target customers regarding your product or service? Which criteria can help you segment them in groups of people having the same interests and behavior? While conducting this deep analysis, we will inev- itably identify seven or eight types of customers with the same contour, motiva- tions, and behavior: those are your *personas*. For instance, if you sell a trendy coffee machine and you have the impression that most of your target customers are into web design and photography, and like the Olympus brand, we can conduct desktop research (have a look at the Internet, magazines, and so on) to get inspired and informed on the topic and then interview one or two experts with very open questions.

Visual search engines help in getting all the important links on a topic—for instance "webdesigner and photography"—in a nutshell. While browsing the most relevant websites, the key is to be open to new visions in order not to ignore 'unconsciously' results that do not fit. If half of the web designer blogs visited talk about photography and many cite Olympus, it is fair to formulate the hypothesis that our web designer *persona* is a photography enthusiast, promotes Olympus, and shares his/her pictures on Flickr.

1.5.2.2 Step 2: Describe Your *Persona*

The next step consists in focusing and doing some more systematic research to make sure no important point has been overlooked. Industry and professional association websites are a good source of information. You might want to do this for the two or three most profitable *personas*.

Here is a list of basic questions that you can complement with questions more specific to your business:

- How old are my customers? How much do they earn? What is their motivation in life?
- What are their job and hobbies? What did they study?
- Do they have family and children? Do they have pets?
- When, where and how do they purchase? How do they use services?
- What are their indoor and outdoor activities?
- When and where do they spend time waiting?
- How do they perceive taste, smell, colors, shapes, sound, texture?

Concerning consumers behavior, if you cannot afford your own survey, you can use analogy. Be careful to understand the context. For instance, if you realize that web designers spend some budget and time decorating their space in Second Life, you can formulate the hypothesis that they might also like decorating their house in real life. Indeed, you discover then that web designers like their home interior and allocate a substantial budget to Villeroy & Boch, Iittala and other funky accessories.

To describe them, the idea is to focus on common points and occurrences. If, for instance, two web designers are called Chris, let us call this Persona Chris. If most of them are 27 years old, let us say he is 27 years old. The idea is to avoid averages and intervals—as they do not help getting a clear picture—and to prefer occurrences.

Giving a name, and sharing the job and hobbies will help identify customers' motivation and their way of thinking, and their own logic. It is then easier to understand and predict their decisions and behavior.

1.5.2.3 Step 3: Validate and Share your *Personas*

The last step consists in testing and refining our vision with experts in contact with clients (call center agents, vendors) to confirm its validity. If a product is intended for web designers, we will not take into account the objection of finance people: they are not in our target! In a business-to-business context, we can easily interview two or three deciders. They will be more than happy to share their thoughts and may even become the champions of our project.

Only at this stage, we will look at competitors in order not to be influenced by them before we have developed a solid vision. If we detect that Dolce Gusto promotes its devices on several websites for web designers, this confirms our vision. The ultimate goal is to find insights competitors did not even think of. We can complement the research by a query in our CRM database: "How many of the registered clients are web designers?"—much more effective than an expensive quantitative survey.

Sharing the vision as much as possible with other departments within the organization (design, communications, sales) helps get input and involvement.

By observing Chris in Second Life and interviewing vendors in contact with him in real life, we identified for instance that he has an estrogen-driven *Hormonal Quotient*^{TM} (HQ) and tolerates some bitterness, and salty taste, but prefers sweet taste. Critical information if we want to deliver the best suited coffee. We will come back to it in the following chapters and show how you can identify the sensory profile and the Hormonal Quotient^{TM} (HQ) your target customers of (Fig. 1.6).

1.5.3 Innovation Funnel or Innovation Matrix?

Once the target consumers and their preferences are roughly identified, we can generate insights. But as there are many options to investigate, the insight generations can quickly become a painful process. People having the market vision list many unfeasible ideas whereas people having the technological knowledge list ideas that do not really sound like benefits for clients. As pointed out in the Innovation Path Matrix—framework focusing on personas rather than on products—firms have many ways to go. They can focus on (Fig. 1.7):

- *Best practice, or imitating innovation*: imitating firms from the same industry is not innovating but is gathering best practice. This activity is useful but not sustainable on its own. Best practice should be gathered in the background to complement a horizontal or vertical innovation path.
  R&D effort: Low. Business Risk: Low.
- *Horizontal innovation*: horizontal innovation consists of the firm looking at how companies from other industries propose products and services to the same *personas* than the ones targeted by the firm. The easiest way is to observe the Personas' User Experience Chain. When dealing with the same Persona, the innovation path is not risky and can lead to radical or business model innovation.
  R&D effort: High. Business Risk: Medium to Low.
- *Vertical innovation*: vertical innovation consists for the firm in having a look at how companies in the same industry propose products and services to different *personas* than their current target. This innovation path is riskier than horizontal innovation in terms of business opportunity—the new target group is unknown—and, in the case of pre-existing solutions, requires an extra development cost to adapt the product to the new Persona. So, the Return on Innovation might be lower. This approach is best suited for start-ups or business units who have the room to shape their organization and business accordingly.
  R&D effort: Medium. Business Risk: High.
- *Exploration*: prospective research consists in looking at what is done in other industries for other *personas*. This innovation path is hazardous and should be conducted in the background to complement a horizontal or vertical innovation strategy. Exploration can be promoted internally. At 3M for instance, employees spend 15% of their working time on the project of their choice (Sameer Kumar 2005).
  R&D effort: High. Business Risk: High.

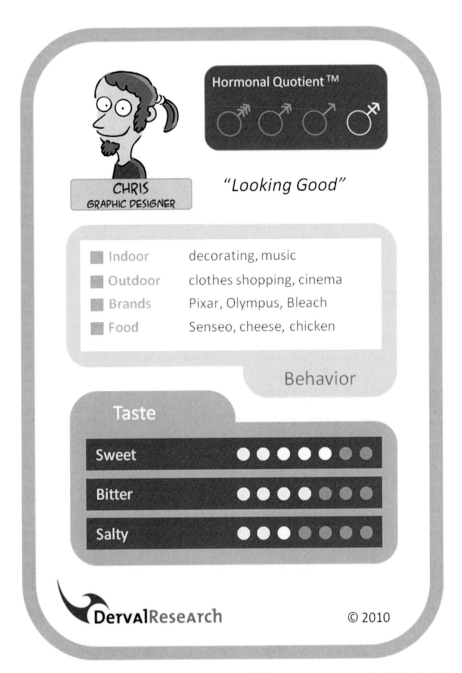

Fig. 1.6 Persona Chris with Hormonal Quotient[TM] (HQ) and taste profile (printed with DervalResearch permission)

Fig. 1.7 Innovation path matrix (Derval and Ardet 2008)

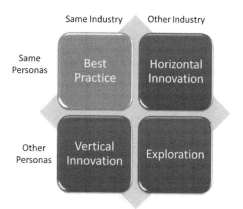

Often a consensus is reached, after many meetings and passionate discussions, on best practice projects consisting in copying competitors. Focusing on the personas rather than watching direct competitors is a right step towards innovation.

Let us take the example of Velib', a groundbreaking innovation in the bike rental industry, and see which personas have a sense of balance.

The Velib' network, an initiative from the Mayor of Paris and financed by advertising revenues generated by partner JC Decaux, is composed of over 20,000 bikes available in 1,500 stations. The vision of Jean-Charles Decaux, President of the outdoor advertising empire JC Decaux, with Velib' was to propose an "Individual Mass Public Transport." And it works—as of today Velib' represents 31 millions trips a year and the number of bikes in Paris has considerably increased since the launch (Derval and Ardet 2008).

Target Personas were people having short trips to do within the city. Not only tourists, but Parisians taking care of their personal administrative stuff and shopping at lunch time. So the typical *personas*, based on studies conducted by the City of Paris and confirmed by a study conducted by the city of Berlin and DervalResearch, would be Kim, waitress (Derval and Menti 2008).

Kim is 29 years old, a waitress, and taking evening classes to become a marketing assistant (Fig. 1.8).

Fig. 1.8 Velib' persona Kim (printed with DervalResearch permission)

She has a good sense of proprioception and of balance (luckily, otherwise she would spill drinks on the clients), enjoys yoga, having a coffee latte with friends, and reading. She lives in Paris and goes to work by metro.

As her agenda is busy, she would love to do her shopping at lunch time, but taking the public transport again with her shopping bags is not a nice perspective.

The product requirements for Velib' were therefore: Easy-to-pick-up and suited for shopping—Kim is not into technologies and she appreciates the shopping basket.

If we apply the Innovation Path Matrix to the bike industry, here is the outcome:

- Best practice or Imitating innovation: adding a shopping basket on the bike.
- Horizontal innovation: by considering Kim's activities and hobbies, and getting inspiration from the retail industry, Velib' designed a bike rental system as easy to use as a shopping cart.
- Vertical innovation: TomTom offering an affordable GPS navigation device for bikers.
- Exploration: designing Bike Caps to protect the saddle from the rain.

In the case of *Velib'*, observing different industries successfully serving their target *persona* led to successful *horizontal innovations*.

1.5.4 Inspiration from Other Industries

The Velib' team considered different options when designing its winning product:

- *The sources of inspiration in the same industry*. During their planning activities, the Velib' team considered *Call-a-Bike*, the bike rental system operated by German railway company *Deutsche Bahn*. They were not convinced by it because users have to call a dedicated phone number to have a bike unlocked. So Velib' decided to develop its own system.
- *The sources of inspiration in related industries was car rental.* "Looking across substitute industries" was a quick-win for Velib' (Kim and Mauborgne 2001). Due to the mass effect, the Parisian firm could even improve the system by offering the users the luxury to take the bike at a station and leave it at another one (there's one every 300 m on average), and this with no extra fee.
- *The most brilliant insight was coming from another industry serving those Personas*: Retail. The most popular 'individual mass transport' system is without any doubt the shopping cart. No wonder that JC Decaux is already advertising on those. The challenge was to apply a similar easy-to-use system to the transport of people, including the billing. Another Kim-friendly example is the award-winning *Velodusche* concept: literally a dishwasher for bikes.

The brief has been met by Velib'. Kim can check around noon the availability of a bike at the nearest Velib' station in real-time at velib.paris.fr. Kim can pick up a bike with her standard metro chipset card. Easier than picking up a shopping cart.

And when she is done, she can leave her new friend on wheels at the Velib' station of her choice and go back to work.

Analyzing the target *personas*, and getting insights from firms serving them in other industries is the key to designing winning innovations, with limited risks.

We saw in this chapter the importance of identifying the best target consumers for our products and how coming to our senses could help. Let us see in Chap. 2 where we can find many of them, and detect profitable markets.

1.6 Take-Aways

Product preferences

- Culture is a temporary local standard that can evolve if better options are proposed.
- Brands are legitimate only because they deliver the right sensory mix.
- Emotion is often an innate response to a sensory stimuli.

Taste

- Individuals have a different perception of the same stimulus.
- Teams developing products are not necessarily representative of their target customers.
- Science can help make reliable business decisions.

Senses

- Millions of sensors are monitoring our behavior.
- The brain manages the sensory input to avoid an overload.
- Emotions like anger, surprise, or disgust are in fact innate responses to a stimulus.

Insights

- Observing consumers is more effective than asking them questions.
- Identifying the job, hobbies, motivation, and behavior of your target consumers helps generate relevant insights.
- Retroductive reasoning is the only way to design groundbreaking innovations.

References

Bartoshuk LM (1994) PTC/PROP tasting: anatomy, psychophysics, and sex effects. Physiol Behav 56(6):1165–1171

Derval D (2009a) Wait Marketing: is it the right moment? DervalResearch, Amsterdam

Derval D (2009b) Hormonal Fingerprint and taste perception. 13th Annual conference of the Society for Behavioral Neuroendocrinology, p 123. Society for Behavioral Neuroendocrinology, East Lansing

Derval D, Ardet N (2008) Wait Marketing applied to vehicle-to-X communications: a framework to open innovation. Marcus Evans, Stockholm

Derval D, Menti M (2008) Survey technology in virtual environments: interview sofas and virtual face-to-face interviews. MRS annual conference. Market Research Society, London

Feldman D (2008) The Coke Zero craze. The diet channel: http://www.thedietchannel.com/node/1739. Accessed 10 Nov 2009

Howard T (2007) Coke finally scores another winner. USA Today: http://www.usatoday.com/money/advertising/adtrack/2007-10-28-coke-zero_N.htm. Accessed 10 Nov 2009

Kim W, Mauborgne R (2001) Creating new market space. In: Harvard business review on innovation. Harvard Business School Press, Boston, pp 1–30

Linehan G (director) (2006) The IT Crowd (Motion Picture)

Marieb EN (2007) Regulation and integration of the body. In: Marieb EN (ed) Human anotomy & physiology, 7th edn. Pearson Education, San Francisco, pp 387–640

Michon, O'Sullivan M, Delahunty C, Kerry J (2009) The investigation of gender-related sensitivity difference in food perception. J Sens Stud 24(6):922–937

Matsumoto D (2009) Facial expressions of emotion are innate, not learned. Journal Personal Social Psychol

Peirce CS (1992) Reasoning and the logic of things: the Cambridge conference lectures of 1898 (Harvard Historical Studies). Harvard University Press, Cambridge

Pinel JP (2007) Basics of biopsychology. Pearson Education, Boston

Ritchie G (director) (2009) Sherlock Holmes (Motion Pictures)

Robyn L (2009) Red Bull invests in X-fighters. Morningadvertiser: http://www.morningadvertiser.co.uk/news.ma/ViewArticle?R=83245. Accessed 10 Nov 2009

Stanford (2009) Charles Sanders Peirce. From standard Encyclopedia of philosophy: http://plato.stanford.edu/entries/peirce/. Accessed 21 Feb 2010

Wipperfurth A (2005) Brand Hijack: marketing without marketing. Portfolio Hardcover, San Francisco

Chapter 2
Detecting Profitable Markets

In this chapter, we show how to detect profitable markets through the *Nintendo Wii* and *DS* revolution. The secrets of sound perception are unveiled with the example of *Shazam* and Dutch Railways (NS). We learn how to leverage sensory knowledge in order to identify profitable markets, in the context of emerging countries, or disruptive innovations.

2.1 Introduction

In this chapter, we find out how to detect profitable markets. We start in Sect. 2.2, by wondering what makes a market more attractive and illustrate this with the sound system case. In Sect. 2.3, We dig into the world of music and learn about consumers' preferences and sensitivities. In Sect. 2.4, we make the link between sensory perception, sense of danger, and the immune system. This will not only help us design user-friendly products but also, as we study in Sect. 2.5, spot great business opportunities (Fig. 2.1).

2.2 What Makes a Market More Attractive? The Sound System Case

Let us see with the sound system case what makes a market attractive. The role of product superiority and competitive benchmarking is reviewed. We also explore consumer barriers and motivations, and why market seizing exercises often go wrong.

D. Derval, *The Right Sensory Mix*, DOI: 10.1007/978-3-642-12093-0_2,
© Springer-Verlag Berlin Heidelberg 2010

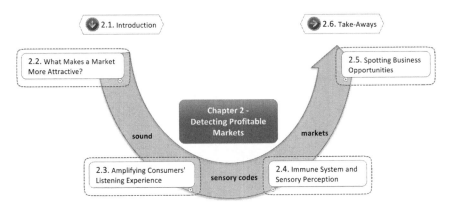

Fig. 2.1 Content of Chap. 2

2.2.1 Product Superiority

My sensory journey brought me to the music industry. Our mission was to help adapt sound systems for different target groups. The big disparities among consumers but also between countries, heavy R&D investments, and a fierce competition presented a challenge.

Music format moved from LP to CD to MP3. Everybody considered this shift as a great improvement and immediately embraced the iPod. Almost everybody— some 'audio-nerds', fascinated by sound reproduction, were still resisting, claiming that the quality of music has been downgraded. This was worth an ethnographic study. In interviews, they reported following disgraces:

- CDs introduce harmonic distortions and limit the dynamic range you can find on LPs—the example of Metallica's "Death Magnetic" is often cited (Anderson 2007).
- MP3 took the horror further by plucking notes out of CDs to make them fit in a file 10 times smaller. The 'perceptual coding' used is supposed to remove only sounds not perceptible to human ears (Jayant et al. 1993).Which humans? Which ears? Those are exactly the questions. What we found out, and will share with you throughout this chapter, is that all ears are not on an equal footing.

2.2.2 Competitive Benchmarking

All companies cannot be as focused on their target consumers as *Apple. Creative Labs* was for a long time reluctant to switch to MP3. They put themselves in a very difficult position but somehow bounced back with their Zen range and attracted many of the 'audio-nerds' of the market, enjoying the file formats available— including FLAC (Free Lossless Audio Codec) an alternative to MP3 that combines fidelity and compression—and other compatibility benefits. Then suddenly, *Creative* launched an iPod clone. Busy copying competition, they left out critical features, upsetting their consumers as we can read on the blog of a Zen fan: "*A device that synchronizes with the PC, not with Bluetooth or Wi-Fi, but with a god fricken cable! What year does Creative think this is?!*" (Dvorak 2009). Benchmarking competitors can lead to wrong positioning if the target consumers are different. Also, it is not an issue if many people dislike a product as long as the existing consumer base still loves it.

2.2.3 Consumers Barriers and Motivations

If we observe iPod users, we understand that their motivation is to enjoy music on the go, while running, doing fitness, or waiting for their train. At home, they have more options. They can listen to the iPod with a practical docking system, switch back to their CD collection, listen to music from their computer, or turn the home theater system on. At home, they also have more constraints. Consumers might have to cope with other family members' desiderata or with neighbors' feedback on their music.

Many men are for instance trying to sneak a home theater system into their home or on the wedding-list, and are facing objections from their wife or future wife (or ex?) because it would not fit nicely in the living room or be too loud. Adding, that she already has to constantly put the volume down!

The dilemma is to satisfy not only the purchaser, or one user, but the whole household. Like in business to business situations where you have to map the purchasing center with the stakeholders—it is critical to identify your champion, here the man, and to provide him with the needed objection-handling script. What he does not suspect yet is that his wife is not putting the volume down just to be annoying.

Did You Know? Noise and Snacking

Research shows that women exposed to stressful noises tend to eat more sweet and salty food (Cousino Klein et al. 2004). No wonder that movies are so loud and popcorn so popular in movie theaters. You can help your wife lose weight just by putting the volume of your sound system down!

2.2.4 The Valley of Illusion

High R&D cost calls for scale saving. You start by then considering new consumer target groups or new countries. Adapting a product to other customers or countries is a stressful process. Whether the existing product is a top or a flop, the key is to understand why. A common pitfall is to consider the potential market as being infinite. In our example, it would be anybody with ears and a wallet. As we saw earlier, some consumers are just not interested in a product whereas others would be ready to sell their mother—let us say their mother-in-law—to get it. Evaluating the attractiveness of a market based on the number of people who consider it as a 'must have' rather than a 'nice to have' has proven to be a very reliable approach, as we will discuss later in this chapter.

For now, we still have to understand why some people put the volume up and others put it down when listening to music.

2.3 Amplifying Consumers' Listening Experience

Let us have a closer look at how our ears work, and see why companies taking into consideration consumers' listening experience are so successful, with the cases of *Shazam* and *Dutch Railways* (*NS*). This will help us evaluate the market attractiveness for sound systems, games, music instruments, ringtones, and make the most of ambient music.

2.3.1 The Secrets of Sound Perception

2.3.1.1 Hearing Spectrum

Sound is a vibration. The number of times a sound vibrates per second is called frequency and is expressed in Hertz (Hz). Loudness, also called amplitude, is a pressure of sound on the inner-ear, measured in decibels (dB).

The human ear can detect sounds between 20 Hz and 20 kHz. Elephants communicate in lower frequencies called infrasound. Bats navigate thanks to higher frequencies called ultrasound (Fig. 2.2).

Captivating, sometimes loud, surrounding, or in the background—sound is very present in our daily lives. When observing our various listening experiences, we can wonder if we all share the same perception of sound. Why, for instance, do some individuals listen to music with the volume up and others with the volume down?

Fig. 2.2 Frequencies detected by human ear (printed with DervalResearch permission)

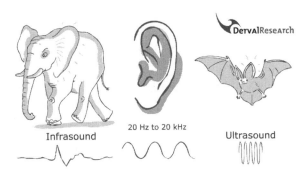

Infrasound   20 Hz to 20 kHz   Ultrasound

2.3.1.2 Otoacoustic Emissions

Twenty-five thousand hair cells, located in our inner ear, help us perceive sound. Each of their stereocilia captures and amplifies a certain frequency (Marieb 2007).

Haircells and stereocilia generate their own noise when amplifying sound. This noise is called otoacoustic emissions (OAE) and can be measured in the ear with a special microphone (Fig. 2.3).

Did You Know? If Ears Could Talk
   Otoacoustic emissions are so unique from one individual to another that feasibility studies are conducted on how to use them as a kind of 'earprint' to identify consumers over the phone (ICBA 2004).

There are two methods used by professionals to assess the hearing spectrum of subjects:

- *Audiogram*: the audiogram is a subjective method for evaluating the hearing spectrum where the subject declares whether or not he hears each frequency played in a headphone. You can test your hearing with our audiogram at www.derval-research.com. Make sure you use a good quality PC sound card and headphone.
- *Otoacoustic emissions*: screening the otoacoustic emissions is an objective method that measures, thanks to a tiny microphone introduced in the inner-ear, how each frequency sent to the inner-ear is amplified.

We decided to validate our hypothesis that some people amplify sound much more that others on 16 Caucasian men in their thirties with no reported hearing issues. We measured the otoacoustic emissions of the 16 volunteers, with a clinical OAE reader provided by Interacoustics, and asked them among other questions (like their favorite music instrument, where they sit at the cinema, their job and hobbies) which sounds they found particularly disruptive (Table 2.1).

We found out that:

- *A same individual can amplify differently bass, speech, and high-pitch sounds.* For instance subject 16 (S16) hears much better high-pitched sounds than speech.

Fig. 2.3 Haircells and stereocilia (printed with DervalResearch permission)

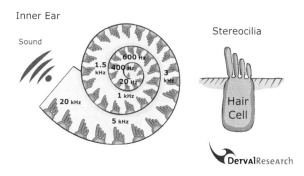

Table 2.1 Otoacoustic emissions variations among individuals (Derval 2010)

Subjects	0.7 kHz Bass	1 kHz	2 kHz Speech	4 kHz	6 kHz High-pitched	10 kHz	12 kHz	Disruptive sounds
S1	−1.0	8.0	26.0	19.0	16.0	23.0	−1.0	Baby
S2	1.0	7.0	17.0	20.0	19.0	12.0	10.0	
S3	2.0	4.0	23.0	21.0	17.0	18.0	4.0	Plates
S4	5.0	14.0	26.0	24.0	23.0	10.0	12.0	High-pitched sound
S5	0.0	8.0	16.0	23.0	21.0	−1.0	6.0	High-pitched sound
S6	−1.0	3.0	4.0	10.0	15.0	16.0	10.0	Train
S7	7.0	1.0	24.0	16.0	22.0	22.0	11.0	Too loud bass
S8	9.0	17.0	31.0	23.0	24.0	20.0	17.0	
S9	6.0	−2.0	12.0	13.0	14.0	0.0	11.0	
S10	9.0	8.0	11.0	9.0	3.0	3.0	7.0	
S11	4.0	9.0	12.0	8.0	2.0	2.0	6.0	
S12	−1.0	6.0	14.0	14.0	6.0	3.0	6.0	
S13	0.0	8.0	28.0	23.0	25.0	38.0	6.0	Mosquito
S14	0.0	11.0	23.0	28.0	39.0	17.0	11.0	Baby
S15	11.0	6.0	17.0	16.0	32.0	16.0	21.0	High-pitched sound
S16	6.0	12.0	17.0	15.0	30.0	21.0	21.0	Klaxon

OAE measurements performed with an Interacoustic OtoRead clinical device by DervalResearch in September 2009. Screening Protocol: TE for [0.7, 1.4] kHz, DP for [2, 12] kHz. Values are expressed in decibels (dB)

- *Some individuals hear a same sound more than four times louder than others.* For instance, subject 14 (S14) hears a baby crying—it is in the 6 kHz area when the baby is angry and 4 kHz when it is happy (so please make them laugh!)—with an intensity of 39 dB, whereas subject 2 (S2) hears it with an intensity of 19 dB. To give you an idea, 20 dB is twice as loud as 10 dB, 30 dB four times louder than 10 dB, and 40 dB is eight times louder than 10 dB.

The otoacoustic emissions in the high frequencies [6, 12] kHz seem to define best the overall hearing sensitivity of an individual. We considered therefore that subjects having a response to a 6 kHz tone:

- >23.0 dB, were super-amplifiers (subjects S13–S16).
- 15.0 dB < response < 23.0 dB, were medium-amplifiers (subjects S1–S7).
- <15.0 dB, were non-amplifiers (subjects S8–S12).

This proposed hearing segmentation has been presented at the 30th International Congress of Audiology in Sao Paulo (Derval 2010).

2.3.1.3 Amplifier Profiles

Our inner-ear works like an amplifier. Depending on their gender, ethnicity, and age, individuals amplify sound in very different ways (Fig. 2.4). We observed for instance that Indians tend to add extra bass whereas Chinese do not like too much

Fig. 2.4 Amplifier profiles (printed with DervalResearch permission)

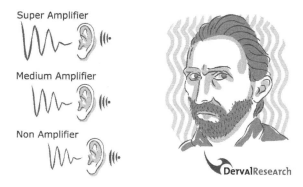

Super Amplifier

Medium Amplifier

Non Amplifier

DervalResearch

'boom-boom' as they call it. As we will see in the next chapter, hormones are greatly involved in explaining such disparities.

Further measurements and observations confirmed following hearing patterns (Table 2.2):

- Super-amplifiers hear very well bass, speech, and perceive high frequencies, like a crying baby (6 kHz), a barking dog, or an airplane, four times louder than non-amplifiers, and two times louder than medium-amplifiers. This group, mainly composed of women, avoids exposure to loud sounds, and favors music and video content in the speech area (1–4 kHz), like pop music and romantic comedies. Bass is still preferred to high-pitch, and high-pitch is tolerated if distortion-free (Fig. 2.5).
- Medium-amplifiers hear very well bass and almost as well high-pitch. They hear less well speech and are therefore sensitive to bass (traffic jam, electronic devices, and background noise)—especially during a conversation. This group enjoys music and video content in the speech area, with some high-pitch accents like alternative rock and action/science fiction movies, and limited bass.
- Non-amplifiers hear speech distinctly and do not hear bass and high-pitch very well. They are therefore very resistant to loudness, and do not mind background noise. They might be sensitive to very specific distortions or sounds like nails or chalk on a blackboard—the type of frequency already used by our ancestors to send alerts. This group, mainly composed of men, enjoys loud music and video content with enhanced bass.

2.3.1.4 Sound Direction

Sounds lower than 80 Hz are difficult to localize. Women are better at locating a sound when it comes from behind and men when it comes from the front.

Men listen with only one side of their brains, while women use both sides. This is also true regarding sound direction: women activate twice as much pixels in their brain to localize a sound source (Maeder et al. 2001).

Table 2.2 Listening preferences by amplifier profiles

	Non-amplifier	Medium-amplifier	Super-amplifier
Bass	Needs to put up the volume to hear bass properly	Sensitive to bass sounds	Sensitive to bass sounds
Speech	Hears speech well	Has difficulties following a conversation with background noise	Is disturbed by surrounding noises
High-pitch	Does not hear high-pitch sounds so well except for alert signals	Hears high-pitched sounds very well	Is very sensitive to high-pitched sounds
Sensitivities	Nail on a chalkboard	All bass sounds	Baby crying, cutlery, klaxon
Favorite instruments	Guitar, saxophone	Piano, Violin	Bass, Cello
OAE at 6 kHz	Under 15 dB	Between 15 and 23 dB	Over 23 dB
Estimated population	25%, more men	50%	25%, more women

Based on the measurements and observations performed by DervalResearch on 200 consumers in France, Belgium, and the Netherlands, from May 2009 to January 2010 (Derval 2010)

Fig. 2.5 Sensitivity to loudness (printed with DervalResearch permission)

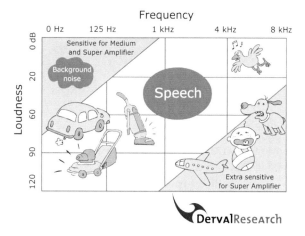

Fig. 2.6 Sound modifiers (printed with DervalResearch permission)

2.3.1.5 Sound Modifiers

Women are more likely to be amplifiers than men. Their hearing sensitivity increases during menstrual cycle and pregnancy. With age, women hear less well low frequencies. Men tend to lose first high frequencies and then might have issues following a conversation.

Factors such as the shape of our ears, our body mass index, and the size of the room we are in will also alter the perceived sound (Fig. 2.6).

Addressing the different consumers' hearing patterns can help propose the right products and services. The transport industry gives us some very good examples.

2.3.2 Dutch Railways (NS), *Music Soothes Waiting Travelers*

Following the example of London buses successfully playing classical music to make travelers feel safer, the London underground is now playing Haydn and Berlioz from dawn to midnight. Interviewed people did not all seem enthusiastic about the play-list and some would like to see the name of the songs currently playing (Fisher 2008). We will see later in this chapter that companies like *Shazam* perfectly grasped this market opportunity.

Many public places look into music as a way to improve consumers' satisfaction and increase the impression of comfort and safety. The Dutch Railways (NS) studied the impact of different types of music tempo on the perception of time spent waiting at the station (Boes and Van Hagen 2010). They segmented their travelers in two main categories according to their motivation:

- 'Must' people, traveling for work (visiting a client, going to the office, on the way back home). They are mainly men.
- 'Lust' people, traveling for leisure (visiting friends, going out). They are mainly women.

The hypothesis formulated is that 'must' people are a bit anxious and therefore looking for a relaxing music (<72 BPM (Beats Per Minute)), whereas 'lust' people might feel bored and are welcoming some more exciting music (>94 BPM).

The survey made by NS among 1,013 travelers highlights for instance that in stressful situations, like peak times, 28% of the respondents would rather not listen to music whereas 34% of them would enjoy classical music. Later in the evening, 75% of the respondents would favor easy listening music. Men showed a clear preference for relaxing music. 'Happy' music played bothered them more than women.

Adapting music to the moment of the day, the affluence, and why not, the train compartment could for sure offer nice development perspectives (Boes and Van Hagen 2010).

> Did You Know? Music Should Come From Our Heart!
> Subjects were asked to adjust the tempo of a song, until they felt comfortable with it.
> The outcome is that they preferred a rhythm closest to their own heartbeat (Iwanaga 1995).

2.3.3 Music Preferences: Are You Pop or Classical?

How can we explain these differences in music preferences? As the way we amplify sound explains how loud we listen to the music, I wondered if we could also explain why some people like pop and others prefer classical music. And this by analyzing the link between our favorite songs and the way we amplify each frequency.

We collected therefore the 2–3 favorite tunes of 3 Caucasian subjects in their thirties—1 medium-amplifier (man), 1 super-amplifier (woman), and 1 non-amplifier (man)—and analyzed the frequencies of their favorite (sometimes least favorite) songs, with the spectrum analyzing software *Spectrum Analyzer Pro Live 2009*, by *Pas Products*. We were then able to compare the frequencies of their favorite music to the otoacoustic emissions of each subject (Table 2.3).

Subject 1 (S1), is a medium-amplifier, who amplifies quite well speech and high-pitched sounds but less good bass sounds. He listens to metal and to alternative rock.

His first favorite tune "Doomed Lover" by My Dying Bride, classified as metal/doom, concentrates the frequency peaks in the bass range [50, 250 Hz] where the subject amplifies the sound the least. On the other hand, in the frequencies higher than 2 kHz, where the subject hears better, the music is softer, it goes down from −20 to −40 dB (Fig. 2.7).

Another favorite tune, "Black Path" by Aereogramme, classified as alternative rock, has a spectrum very similar to the metal song analyzed earlier, with a peak around 110 Hz (Fig. 2.8).

Analyzing frequencies is more reliable than referring to music genres.

Subject 2 (S2) is a super-amplifier and amplifies very well sound in bass, even more in speech, and almost too much in high frequencies. She enjoys punk/alternative rock, but not all songs as we will see.

Table 2.3 Otoacoustic emissions in bass, speech, and high-pitch frequencies

Subject	Gender	0.7 kHz Bass	1 kHz	2 kHz Speech	4 kHz	6 kHz High-pitched	10 kHz	12 kHz	Amplifier profile
S1	M	−1.0	8.0	26.0	19.0	16.0	23.0	−1.0	Medium-amplifier
S2	F	12.0	14.0	26.0	25.0	33.0	23.0	16.0	Super-amplifier
S3	M	6.0	−2.0	12.0	13.0	14.0	0.0	11.0	Non-amplifier

OAE measurements performed with an Interacoustics OtoRead clinical device by DervalResearch in September 2009. Screening Protocol: TE for [0.7, 1.4] kHz, DP for [2, 12] kHz. Values are expressed in decibels (dB)

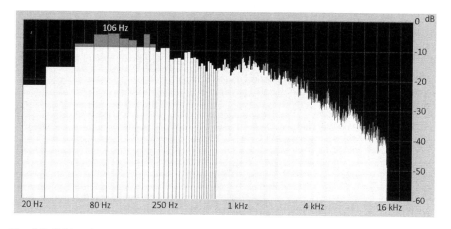

Fig. 2.7 Subject 1, spectrum analysis: "Doomed Lover" by My Dying Bride

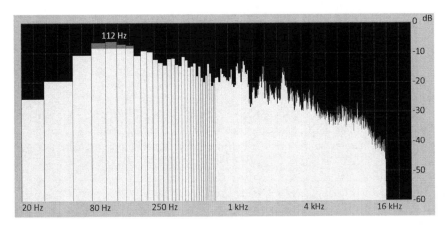

Fig. 2.8 Subject 1, spectrum analysis: "Black Path" by Aereogramme

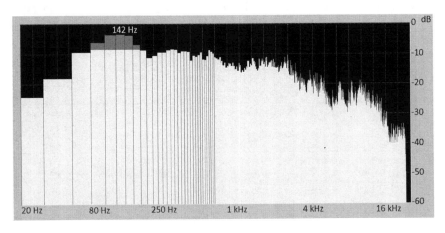

Fig. 2.9 Subject 2, spectrum analysis: "Give It Away" by the Red Hot Chili Peppers

The favorite tune, "Give It Away" from the Red Hot Chili Peppers is focusing on the bass sounds. Which is perfect for our super-amplifier (Fig. 2.9).

We were then curious to know about a song irritating her. She cited "My Immortal" from Evanescence, also alternative rock but with a very different spectrum: the peak is around 2 kHz, in the speech area, where the subject amplifies very well (Fig. 2.10).

Again, a music genre can include very different types of songs.

Our last subject (S3) is a non-amplifier and does not amplify bass and low speech so well.

The peak of his favorite tune "Better be home soon" by Crowded House, happens around 1 kHz—exactly at the frequency where there is a hole in the subject's hearing spectrum, with his lowest response to noise: −2 dB only (Fig. 2.11)!

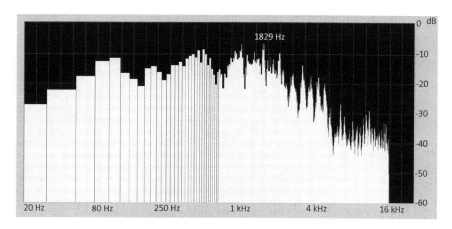

Fig. 2.10 Subject 2, spectrum analysis: "My Immortal" by Evanescence

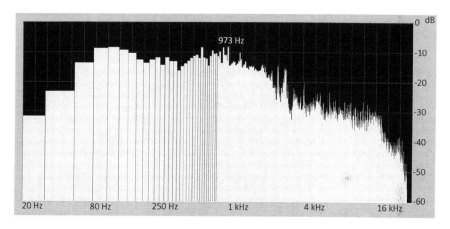

Fig. 2.11 Subject 3, spectrum analysis: "Better Be Home Soon" by Crowded House

After all, this makes sense: why would you listen to music that is attacking your ears? In the favorite as well as in the least favorite music, the rhythm, the singer, and the lyrics play a role, but in many cases it is just about wrong or right frequencies.

Did You Know? Favorite Music Therapy

About 17% of the population is bothered by Tinnitus, a permanent ringing in the ear (Jastreboff 2008). The latest treatment discovered in Germany is using people's favorite music as a healing method. Subjects play a special version of their favorite music, cleaned from the frequencies posing problem, 12 hours a day. Tinnitus seems to be caused by cortical neurons overreacting to certain frequencies, due to an accidental loud exposure. Just by giving the faulty neurons a break for one year, and only exciting their neighbours in charge of other frequencies (this process is called "lateral inhibition"), the subjects perceive a huge improvement.

2.3.4 Shazam *Music: You Name It!*

Another example of breakthrough linked to music and hearing is *Shazam*.

The one thing I really liked while listening to the radio in the car is that the audio system was able to display the title of the awesome song they just played. The Radio Data System (RDS) or Radio Broadcast Data System (RBDS) is using some spare radio frequencies to send bits of useful information. Other popular services are real-time traffic information alerts. *Shazam* provided this service on our mobile phones (iPhone, Android, Nokia, and more), enabling us to explore music on-the-go.

The principle is quite easy:

- You open *Shazam* on your phone.
- You point your device towards the song you want to identify.
- The program builds an 'audio fingerprint' of the tune, compares it with its database of over eight million tracks and displays the cover of the closest 'audio fingerprint' found.
- And this in a couple of seconds.
- Most incredible is: it actually works! I identified the last Jonas Brother's hit.

All this awesomeness is on top of that for free. For now. Apparently Shazam is introducing new on-demand advertising solutions, probably in a quest for break-even. The commission on the MP3 sales generated consecutively to the identification of the tune may not be sufficient to cover the R&D developments. Maybe they will opt for some kind of identification placement: "This song was identified for you by *Quaker*?" Recent exciting features include an integration with Last.fm and the possibility to see if the artist you just discovered is on tour soon or nearby (Evan 2010).

The firm uses its software as a smart distribution channel to reach and interact with over 15 million users, as of today. Being able to link music preferences with the mobile owner opens a realm of opportunities. Also the identification requests happen to be excellent predictors of imminent market hits and the whole industry is keeping an eye on the *Shazam* Tag Chart—just saw Adam Lambert in the top 20!

2.3.5 Amplifier Profiles: Business Applications

Based on our amplifier profiles, latest OAE screening methodologies, and sound identification algorithms, we can imagine following amazing new products:

1. Automatic equalizers proposing the best bass/speech/high-pitch mix based on consumers' otoacoustic emissions.
2. Filtering systems that make sure ambient music playing in hotels, stations, and lounges are suited for every type of amplifier.
3. Ringtones and alarm systems adapted to super, medium, and non-amplifiers.
4. Tunes recommendation based on otoacoustic emissions and heartbeat.
5. Acoustic diets limiting snacking by decreasing the ambient noise.

2.4 Immune System and Sensory Perception

Hypersensitivity to sound, and other stimuli, seems linked to our immune system. The study of disorders like autism and the associated sensory sensitivity tells us a lot about regular consumers' perception. Understanding which signals are associated with dangerous situations will help develop user-friendly products.

2.4.1 The Tenth Sense: the Sense of Danger

Our most instinctive sense is probably the sense of danger. That is the one supposed to alert us on risky situations.

Our *immune system* for instance acts like a bouncer and will not let in a quidam with the wrong dress code. In this *innate defense system,* the filtering decision occurs instantly, the criteria being "does he/she fit the club or not?". We also have a second security barrier inside, the *adaptive defense system*, that recalls past events and says, after a while "wait a minute, you were the one leaving without paying last week: out!".

When we think of invaders, bacteria and viruses come to our mind. In some circumstances, relatively harmless visitors like toasted bread and roasted coffee can endanger our immune system. The chemical *Maillard reaction*, that occurs when you heat foods containing sugars, and the advanced glycation endproducts (AGE) they produce are responsible for chronic inflammatory diseases such as Crohn's disease and colitis, diabetes, and delayed type hypersensitivity (DTH). This happens in cases of deficiency of RAGE, the receptor for these advanced glycation endproducts. This receptor is, according to recent observations critical for maintaining the immune tolerance of organs challenged by external stimuli. Not only RAGE senses danger but it seems to directly modulate our behavior, too (Nawroth 2007).

This link between the immune system and sensory perception could explain why some individuals are hypersensitive, and overloaded by external stimuli.

Did You Know? When Plants Are Freaking Out!

  Tobacco plants too have feelings. When sagebrush plants got eaten up by hungry beetles, researchers observed that all the nearby tobacco plants started to produce in their leaves a toxic chemical to protect themselves against the invaders (Karban et al. 2004). This poison is called nicotine.

2.4.2 Why Would Spock Hate Yellow?

An intriguing case of sensory overload is observed in people suffering from Asperger syndrome. This form of autism, situated on the light side of the Autism Spectrum Conditions (ASC), is now detected, for instance in the UK, in one child out of 100.

The character Spock from Star Trek is often depicted as an Asperger: "*I quickly learned that my husband and Spock had a lot in common. My husband could have been the one stating the phrase that's "highly illogical" because emotion didn't play a role in any decision he made. He also became incensed when people made the same mistakes over and over. He felt that people should learn from their mistakes and retain the information for life (just like Spock's brain). Honestly, how many people do you know who still remember their locker combinations from elementary school?*" (Pratinfield 2010)

Aspies, as they are called, are over-sensitive to sound. In most cases, they suffer from hyperacusis: a noise of 65 dB—which corresponds to a loud conversation—will already hurt them, when average people can stand up to 130 dB without any issue. They suffer from anxiety, and are also sensitive to taste and smell. In his last Bollywood movie, Shahrukh Khan plays an Aspie. An incredible scene is when horrified by the yellow jacket his love, played by Kajol, wears, he just runs away (Johar 2010). Indeed, people suffering from Asperger are so sensitive that the yellow color is much too bright for their eyes.

In her book, Jen Birch, diagnosed at 43, tells her story and how she was reluctant as a child to eat vegetables, how bad her sense of balance was when she was trying to learn riding a bike, how she could not make an emotional difference between horror movies and reality (even if she was told it was fiction), and even how clothing was hurting her. For a long time, people thought autistic children did not like contact and hugs for 'psychological' reasons (here we go again!). It appears, however, that in fact they are just over-sensitive to touch (Birch 2003). The disorder was thought to be less common among girls but it looks like they were just under-diagnosed because their symptoms differ from boys: they speak more, are shy or sometimes rebel, and obsessed by more common topics, so that they can get unnoticed.

Did You Know? Einstein socks

   Asperger sufferers are very sensitive to textures and struggle very often to find seamless socks, that feel nice on the toes. Maybe a new market for Blacksocks.com we will study in Chap. 4? As Einstein could not speak fluently at age 9 and attended, years later, his induction ceremony to become an American citizen sockless, it is likely that he was suffering from a form of autism (Fattig 2007).

2.4.3 What is the Difference Between a Nerd?

You may now wonder: "*If Spock is my favorite character in Star Trek, do I fall into some of the Autism Spectrum Conditions (ASC)?*" If chitchat bothers you, if you find it difficult to make new friends or to keep a conversation going, if you know everything about a topic, the answer might well be yes. Believe it or not but while writing this section I checked my level of autism with the test developed by Cambridge's Autism Research Centre and scored 33. A score higher than 32 is a good indicator of some form of ASC, and the average for 'normal' people is 16.4. First, I had a couple of drinks, and then I thought that bordering the Autism spectrum was not that big of an issue after all, as long as people know about it. That's why I decided to do my coming out: we all have a little nerd inside:)

If you have a doubt now, you can take the test and check your friends and family at www.betterimmunesystem.org.

Did You Know? Californian Dream and Autism

In the US, the autism rate is increasing in California, to such an extent—it went up from 5 to 12 cases per 1,000—that the federal government ordered research to find out the causes. The conclusion was: "*Without evidence for an artificial increase in autism cases, we conclude that some, if not all, of the observed increase represents a true increase in cases of autism in California, and the number of cases presenting to the Regional Center system is not an overestimation of the number of children with autism in California.*" (The M.I.N.D. Institute 2002). Wait a minute, where is the Silicon Valley again?

By studying supersensitive individuals, we get a better understanding of some common human perception traits, that can be used as guidelines when designing new products and services.

2.4.4 Sensory Alert Codes and Product Design

Sensors are our alarm system. And even if we all have a different perception of taste and of sound—we see later that it is also true for smell, touch, and vision— some stimuli are perceived universally. They are synonymous with danger.

2.4.4.1 Taste and Danger

The bitter taste of vegetables is due to toxins—the plants must secrete them hoping it will prevent them from being eaten (like with the tobacco plants seen earlier). And it works! Our taste receptors are able to detect the presence of these glucosinolates in natural food. In fact, all the bitter vegetables do not contain this poison: endive and spinach seem safe, but beware of watercress or radish. Experiments with PTC strips showed that tasters perceived vegetables containing glucosinolates 60% more bitter than non-tasters but that both groups perceived safer bitter vegetables in the same way. The research mentions that it is critical for people having thyroid insufficiency to avoid those 'bad bitter' vegetables (Sandell and Breslin 2006). You remember our autistic friends reluctant to eat vegetables? They should listen to their wise taste buds because autism is actually due to hypothyroidism (Gillberg et al. 1992)! The elegance of nature.

So when developing pharmaceutical or food products, making sure the level of bitterness is acceptable for the target consumers is an important step.

Table 2.4 Top 20 disgusting sounds (Cox 2008)

Rank	Disgusting sound	Rank	Disgusting sound
1	Vomiting	11	Tasmanian devil
2	Microphone feedback	12	Cough
3	Multiple babies	13	Cat spitting
4	Train brakes	14	Mobile phone rings
5	Seesaw	15	Creaky door
6	Violin	16	Barking mad dog
7	Whoopee cushion	17	Sniff
8	Baby cry	18	Fingernails on chalkboard
9	Soap opera argument	19	Polystyrene
10	Mains hum	20	Dentist's drill

2.4.4.2 Sound and Danger

It was believed that the sound of a nail on the chalkboard was the most annoying sound ever. Over 400,000 people from Australia, Africa, Middle East, North America, Europe, and South America listened to 34 sounds via the Internet and ranked them from the most to the least horrible. Here are 17 noises considered even more atrocious than a nail on the chalkboard, in this top 20 disgusting sounds, featuring seesaws, violin, train brakes, multiple babies, and vomiting (Table 2.4).

In fact, irritating sounds vary depending on the amplifier profile of the consumer of course. People amplifying more 4 kHz sounds suffer with chainsaw, cutlery noises, and coughing (coughing is much louder than we would expect!), at 6 kHz you will be more sensitive to baby cry, and around 500 Hz to electronic devices. The 'multiple babies' report is symptomatic of a non-amplifier: he/she starts getting annoyed only when a regiment of babies is screaming. Not listed are the car horns and other alarms, especially in the morning!

> Did You Know? Alarm for Senior People
> A promising market is the one of alarms for senior people. Most of the alarms are high-pitched, but that is exactly the part of the hearing spectrum many seniors lose first. A patent has been registered for an alarm you can adjust to the frequency that works best for you.

2.4.4.3 Vision and Danger

Concerning colors and shapes, the advertising industry is probably the best example of what not to follow. They use all the codes of danger to attract consumers' attention: red, yellow, and movements. And it works in the way you notice the message—you have no choice, it is jumping at your face. The question is: How receptive are people when they are attacked by a brand? Luckily firms can use other approaches to get noticed, like communicating at the right moment with *Wait Marketing*. And interacting with customers while they are bored waiting (Derval 2009). So unless you run emergency services, avoid those long wavelength colors as they arrive directly on the focal point of the eye, as we will see in Chap. 5.

In terms of shapes, we are more naturally attracted to human faces. Putting pictures of people on your website and products can help to create a connection with the consumer without being aggressive.

2.4.4.4 Smell and Danger

Incense smoke and other scents including airborne contaminants, can provoke a violent reaction called "odor-induced panic attack" (Greene and Kipen 2002). So if you plan to put incense sticks in your shop or decorate your restaurant with thousands of nice candles, check first if your target consumers are sensitive to chemicals!

2.4.4.5 Touch and Danger

A light touch is an alert code. It allows you to detect a mosquito landing on your arm, or a pickpocket visiting your purse. A sudden change in temperature constitutes a warning, too.

I assume that you do not plan to send painful stimuli to your clients, right? So the key point to remember is that: strong foods like menthol or chili, loud sounds in sensitive frequencies, bright lights, chemical perfumes, and sudden tactile signals can hurt.

Now that we have all the tools to develop user-friendly products, let us see how to develop very popular ones and follow the example of the *Nintendo Wii*.

2.5 Spotting Business Opportunities

Understanding target consumers' perceptions and codes is key for developing good products. We show with the *Nintendo* case that having a look at non-consumers can unlock huge market opportunities. We also show that evaluating the potential market based on 'must have' customers and analyzing the substitution products they currently use is the road to successful opportunity and feasibility studies.

2.5.1 Consumers versus Non-Consumers

As seen previously with the Red Bull case (Wipperfurth 2005), creating a new profitable market is the best business opportunity you can dream of. Millions of customers waiting for you, no competition: a *blue ocean* of opportunities (Kim and Mauborgne 2001). Why would you indeed fight on prices and features with other firms when you can just set up the rules and standards of a new product category?

The only thing you have to do is to find this disruptive innovation. Because it works. Even in overcrowded markets like video games. *Nintendo* just proudly announced that *Nintendo Wii* is now the best-selling hardware in the history of video games with over 67 million devices sold since the launch in 2006. *Nintendo DS* sold over 125 million consoles (Nintendo Co. Ltd 2010). With hits like Super Mario Bros, Wii Sports Resort, Just Dance, and Wii Fit Plus, the company is the uncontested leader in the video game market and has created a new market, making the most of technological sensors and human senses.

But what about Xbox and PlayStation? Let us turn back the clock and see what happened. The battle between Nintendo, Microsoft, and Sony, was so far won by Sony and its fast processing and high definition PlayStation (Farhoomand 2009). Video gamers were mainly men mastering racing, fighting, or arcade games and expert in maneuvering vibrating joysticks. The only way to convert the hardcore gamers was increased performance. Until that special day, when someone at Nintendo decided to look at the market differently and saw huge opportunities. For sure, he must have used a *positioning map*!

Positioning map is a powerful tool used by leading companies but not very well documented in the literature. Here is the one I designed on the video game market a couple of months before the launch of the Wii Fit. As you will realize soon, everything is predictable, with the right data and hypothesis.

The *positioning map* will help you understand your personas, as well as who your direct and indirect competitors are, and you will see the potential and opportunities for your product on the market. It replaces the traditional company SWOT analysis that lists the general strengths, weaknesses, opportunities, and threats, as it is more effective to assess a company's competitive advantage for each and every persona (Fig. 2.12).

Here is how you can build your positioning map in three steps:

2.5.1.1 Step 1: Identify the Groups of Customers that Are Relevant to Your Business

- *Personas*: In the pre-Wii era, gamers were mainly bachelors and nerds (as a reminder, I myself fall in this category, so no offense). Let us take them as our rough personas for now. So bachelors spend most of the time having drinks with friends, playing pool, doing fitness, going to the cinema, and playing Xbox. Nerds are more at home alternating between Home Cinema and PlayStation, more technical than the Xbox.
- *Competitors*: Direct competitors would be Xbox and PlayStation. Indirect competitors would be pubs, pool, cinema, and fitness.

2.5.1.2 Step 2: Find the Relevant Axes

- *Differentiating criteria*: Best is to start with the existing customers: what is the most important for them? In the example of Nintendo Wii, the haptic

Fig. 2.12 Nintendo Wii
positioning map (printed with
DervalResearch permission)

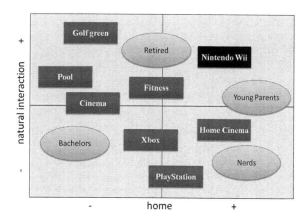

interface—understand by that the natural movements you use to give instruc-
tions to the machine—and the fact you can enjoy entertainment at home are
specific to the Wii. At the same time these criteria help differentiate the nerds—
more at home and keen on a technical user interface (UI)—from bachelors more
outside and not against a more user-friendly UI. We assumed here that bachelors
and nerds were two distinct groups, they are both single but only one is in the
market! These are the two axes of your map. Note that price is never a valid
criteria as it does not help segment your customers: the ones who cannot pay, are
simply not in the target.

- *Relative position*: We can now place the personas on the map according to their
sensitivity to each criteria. For instance, bachelors like going out more than
nerds and are therefore more on the left side of the map. We can also position
the substitution products—the direct and indirect competitors close to the
concerned consumer: For nerds, the direct competitor can be PlayStation, and
the indirect competitor a Home Cinema Theatre.

2.5.1.3 Step 3: Reveal Market Opportunities

The idea is then to find other market opportunities by using retroduction, our
Sherlock Holmes reasoning.

What about using the substitution product to find other personas and then go
back to the product to see which disruptive innovation would suit them best?

So let us start with cinema: who else can we find there? Senior people, probably. Indeed, as young parents are at home busy with baby powder. Talking about
young parents, they are watching Home Cinema Theatre too, like nerds. If we add
retired and young parents on the map, we will suddenly have a vision: Wii Fit!!

Let us have a drink, we are done.

The positioning map helps you to identify blue oceans, adapt products to new
target customers, and design disruptive innovations.

Note that the perceptual map you may encounter is another concept: you ask consumers to tell how they perceive your brand and then you just put their feedback on a map.

2.5.2 Must Have versus Nice to Have

Having a vision, based on observation and reasoning (if I hear the word "intuition" once again, I leave this book!) is a good start, but we now need to make sure that the new market is profitable. To validate the expected revenues, I propose to validate the needs. The idea is that if a consumer thinks a product is a 'must have', he or she will buy it. It is as easy as that. On the other hand, if it is a 'nice to have' then there might be a gap between the purchasing intentions and the actual revenues—a gap called "market flop".

Let us take the retired and young parents consumer groups. For which group is the product a 'must have'?

- Young parents just discovered the magic world of baby powder and 6 kHz sounds. They are a bit stuck at home. They could, of course, invite friends to come over for a movie night but they lost them all the year after birth during which they did not give any signs of life to anybody, the last stimulus received being an atrocious home-made baby announcement card. A Wii would be an alternative to 'couch potatoing' and might even help them make new friends!
- Retired people enjoy their family from a distance and try to travel or occupy their garden as much as possible. Having a Wii would be nice but maybe more for their children and grand-children.

Which segment would you focus on?

We could go for the young parents. As it seems that the retired people are a bit more outside. Also they have more difficulty with reading, less memory (will they remember where they put the Wii control?) Wait a minute, what about designing a special *Nintendo DS* for them that we could call *Brain Age*? Or why not go a step further and include other sensors in the Wii in order to help senior citizen monitor their health? Here you go, it's raining market opportunities.

Did You Know? DS for Seniors
    While I was editing this book, Nintendo announced a new DS model for seniors with Brain Age pre-installed, a bigger screen, and a stylus that resembles more closely a regular pen. You can truly spot opportunities with this positioning map! (Nintendo 2010)

2.5.3 Substitution Products and Market Attractiveness

Back to our young parents. We started with this rough consumer segment, but it is now time to analyze deeper the related personas. This will enable us to evaluate substitution products and market attractiveness.

Let us assume our first Persona Chris, who we studied in Chap. 1, lives with Marcia, a young researcher, and they just had their second child. Marcia is testosterone-driven, we will come back to this in next chapter, and very much into LEGO®, innovations, and just bought a colorful Acer netbook. She visits pop and rock concerts, but always wears ear-plugs as she is a super-amplifier. They both like to have fun but do not want to spend time reading a 100-page user guide before using a system. They heard of the Wii and were intrigued by the natural interaction and also the white design, very different from the Xbox and PlayStation format. The good news is that they are not already equipped with a competitors' solution. What about indirect competitors? They were thinking of buying a new design sofa. On the other hand, with the small children, it might not be the right moment.

Chris and Marcia are clearly trendsetters. They are interested by games, but also fitness and why not some yoga. If other consumer groups are also in the target, let's also go for the Wii Fit. We can now evaluate how many Chris and Marcia households are in the market and plan to convert at least 80% of them, admitting that 20% might have decided to buy the sofa in spite of our warning (Fig. 2.13).

2.5.4 Opportunity or Feasibility Study?

An opportunity study will be needed to validate the previous hypotheses.

We could be tempted to evaluate our Wii opportunity for new young parents in this way:

- There are 10 million young parents households.
- We are realistic and think we will convert 5% of them.
- So our expected sales are 500,000 units.

What is wrong here? The flaws are that, if we assume our product is a 'must have' for young parents, then we should convert them all (or 80% of them because of the sofa). If only some of them are interested, then we have to identify this 5% subgroup.

For international products, it is critical to quantify how many households like Chris and Marcia are present per country.

Contrary to the accepted wisdom, the opportunity study must be detailed enough to not miss a critical aspect of the project. Imagine Nintendo making a whole study on the opportunity to launch the *Wii Vitality Sensor*—that will keep track of a user's heart rate—including the patent for the system, the design, and they discover at feasibility stage only that they need the recommendation of doctors and therapists to convert their personas, with all the associated costs of clinical testing.

The viability of a project is linked to its conformity to the company's strategy and to:

- *The expected revenues*: for which personas is the product a "must have", how many are they, what are they willing to pay? What could they spend their money on, instead?
- *The costs*: what are the main fixed and variable costs?

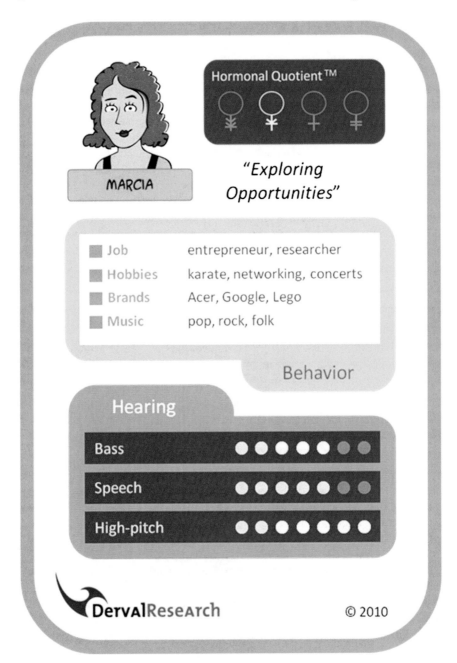

Fig. 2.13 Hormonal Quotient^{TM} (HQ) of Marcia (printed with DervalResearch permission)

The feasibility study consists in describing in detail how to manufacture the peripheral and approach health professionals.

If you take all these steps, you will for sure spot great business opportunities! In this chapter we saw how to detect and even create profitable markets. In Chap. 3, we will see how we can accurately predict the market response.

2.6 Take-Aways

Attractive markets

- Some countries or markets have more of your ideal customers.
- Households are complex purchasing centers.
- A product can be disliked by many people as long as it is loved by its target consumers.

Sound

- Some people hear a crying baby four times louder than others.
- Favorite music has the right tempo and frequency.
- Super, medium, and non-amplifiers amplify bass, speech, and high-pitch in different ways.

Immune system

- Hypersensitivity is linked to our immune system.
- Products like toasted bread or roasted coffee can become toxic.
- To make user-friendly products, let us avoid stimuli perceived as a danger.

Business opportunities

- Observing non-consumers can unlock huge business opportunities.
- Understanding substitution products is a good way to find new clients.
- Designing a positioning map will help you spot these blue oceans.

References

Anderson T (2007) When vinyl is better than CD. Available from Tim Anderson's ITWriting: http://www.itwriting.com/blog/106-when-vinyl-is-better-than-cd.html. Accessed 23 February 2010
Birch J (2003) Congratulation! it's Asperger syndrome. Jessica Kingsley Publisher, London
Boes E, Van Hagen M (2010) Stations? Daar zit muziek in! In: European transport conference 2010, Glasgow
Cousino Klein L, Faraday M, Quigley K, Grunberg N (2004) Gender differences in biobehavioral aftereffects of stress on eating, frustration, and cardiovascular responses. J Appl Soc Psychol 34(3):538–562
Cox T (2008) Scraping sounds and disgusting noises. Appl Acoust 69(12):1195–1204
Derval D (2009) Wait Marketing: is it the right moment? DervalResearch, Amsterdam

Derval D (2010) Hormonal Fingerprint and sound perception: a segmentation model to understand and predict individuals' hearing patterns based on otoacoustic emissions, sensitivity to loudness, and prenatal exposure to hormones. In: 30th International Congress of Audiology-ICA 2010. The International Society of Audiology, Sao Paulo

Dvorak (2009) Creative ZEN X-Fi2 preview: has creative lost its fricken mind?! Available from Dvorak Uncensored: http://www.dvorak.org/blog/2009/09/22/creative-zen-x-fi2-preview-has-creative-lost-its-fricken-mind/. Accessed 23 February 2010

Evan J (2010). Shazam for iPhone gets Last.fm, ticketing and more... Available from 9to5mac: http://www.9to5mac.com/bam_bam_shazam_34889. Accessed 23 February 2010

Farhoomand A (2009) Nintendo's disruptive strategy: implications for the video game industry. The University of HongKong, HongKong

Fisher N (2008) Classical music is a big hit on the London underground. Available from Times Online: http://entertainment.timesonline.co.uk/tol/arts_and_entertainment/music/article3284419.ece. Accessed 24 February 2010

Gillberg I, Gillberg C, Kopp S (1992) Hypothyroidism and autism spectrum disorders. J Child Psychol Psychiatry Allied Discipl 33(3):531–542

Greene G, Kipen H (2002) The vomeronasal organ and chemistry sensitivity: a hypothesis. Environ Health Perspect 110(4):655–661

ICBA (2004) Using otoacoustic emissions as a biometric. In: First international conference on biometric authentication. Springer, Berlin, pp 1–34

Iwanaga M (1995) Relationship between heart rate and preference for tempo of music. Percept Motor Skills 81:435–440

Jastreboff P (2008) Tinnitus & Hyperacusis Center. Available from Emory University Atlanta: http://www.tinnitus-pjj.com/. Accessed 24 February 2010

Jayant N, Johnston J, Safranek R (1993) Signal compression based on models of human perception. IEEE, pp 1385–1422

Johar K (Director) (2010) My name is Khan [Motion Picture]

Karban R, Huntzinger M, McCall A (2004) The specificity of eavesdropping on sagebrush by other plants. Ecology 1846–1852

Kim W, Mauborgne R (2001) Creating new market space. In: Harvard Business Review on innovation. Harvard Business School Press, Boston, pp 1–30

Maeder P, Meuli R, Adriani M, Bellmann A, Fornari E, Thiran JP, Pittet A, Clarke S (2001) Distinct pathways involved in sound recognition and localization: a human fMRI study. Neuroimage 14(4):802–816

Marieb EN (2007) Regulation and integration of the body. In: Marieb EN (ed) Human anatomy and physiology, 7th edn. Pearson Education, San Francisco, pp 387–640

Nawroth P (2007) RAGE, a receptor sensing for danger. In: Ninth international symposium on the Maillard reaction. International Maillard Reaction Society, Munich, p. 38

Nintendo (2010) Nintendo reveals hardware and software lineup for the first half of 2010. Available from Nintendo: http://www.nintendo.com/whatsnew/detail/xfWC6drtSlzaYXjDmtuf7MeuI2Uf94vb. Accessed 14 March 2010

Nintendo Co. Ltd (2010) Financial results debriefing. Nintendo, Tokyo. http://www.nintendo.com/whatsnew/detail/xfWC6drtSlzaYXjDmtuf7MeuI2Uf94vb

Pratinfield M (2010) My husband and son have Asperger's symptoms. Available from all about Aspergers symptoms: http://allaboutaspergerssymptoms.com/my-husband-has-aspergers-symptoms. Accessed 24 February 2010

Sandell M, Breslin P (2006) Variability in a taste-receptor gene determines whether we taste toxins in food. Curr Biol 16(48):792

Wipperfurth A (2005) Brand hijack: marketing without marketing. Portfolio Hardcover, San Francisco

Chapter 3
Predicting Consumers' Behavior

In Chap. 3, we study the predictive power of hormones with the Hormonal Quotient™ (HQ). The biological mechanisms between sensory stimuli and consumers' behavior are clarified with the success stories of *Häagen Dazs*. You will explore the world of smell, and the multisensory perception inspired by examples of daily life and the *Sofitel Amsterdam The Grand* case.

3.1 Introduction

In this chapter, we show that predicting consumers' behavior is so much better than just understanding them. In Sect. 3.2 we analyze how well a product will sell with the launch of a detergent in India. This brings us to the world of fragrances and we contemplate in Sect. 3.3 why some products pass the consumers' smell test and others do not. We then explore in Sect. 3.4 genetics and hormones and find out that there are more common points between male, female, and chicken than we would expect. These findings will inspire us in Sect. 3.5 to better target consumers with powerful predictive tools (Fig. 3.1).

3.2 How Well Will a Product Sell? The Detergent Case

My next sensory adventure inspired me to discover and analyze the world of smell. The mission this time was "Let us assume we decided to launch our successful cleaning product in India. How do we need to adapt it? And can we predict the sales?"

3.2.1 The Purchasing Intention Trap

The company does some projections based on their sales in Europe. The way companies usually do this, is to ask potential consumers: "Hi, we are launching this product, would you buy it?" In some sophisticated cases, they even let

D. Derval, *The Right Sensory Mix*, DOI: 10.1007/978-3-642-12093-0_3,
© Springer-Verlag Berlin Heidelberg 2010

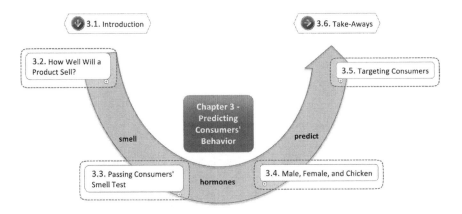

Fig. 3.1 Content of this Chap. 3

consumers try the product, which is already a bit better. A pharmaceutical group, for instance, knew that a medicine would soon not be reimbursed, and generic products being cheaper, they were wondering which part of their clients would still buy it. The conclusion of the survey was clear: about 80% would remain loyal to the brand. Guess what? 80% of the clients switched to generic products. The two main reasons for this wrong forecast are that: (a) if you ask people nicely, most of them will answer yes, as they do not want to break the interviewer's heart, (b) the people asked were age and gender-matched but not exactly the same persona they targeted. So my answer was yes, we can predict consumers' behavior, but only if we understand exactly how they work, and identify their sensory context.

3.2.2 A Tendency to Overperform

One of the major engineering biases is—we had a good demonstration of this with the Nintendo Wii case—is to focus on performance. So it is like whoever says "cleaning products" is really saying "washing performance".

Do not get me wrong—I do not say a cleaning product should not wash (it can well be useful), but overperformance is just expensive and does not help you win a market. This occurs often when you make a benchmark with all the competitors in the market. You put all the features you think of in an Excel file, you evaluate them and your objective is to be better on each of them. But as we analyzed with Nintendo, for each persona you have specific substitution products and criteria.

I decided to review them for this cleaning product.

3.2.3 Importance of the Sensory Context

The first question that came to my mind was "What do we know about the target consumers' clothing, and eating habits?" It sounded weird during the meeting, as it usually happens when I start retroducting. It might sound funny, but you probably do not need the same performance if you wear white clothes, made of difficult to wash textiles, eat tomato ketchup every day, and tend to be clumsy.

The second question I wondered about was "What do we compare the performance to?" Competing cleaning products tend to make white clothes a bit grey after a certain number of washings, let's say 7. Interesting, but some people in India use soap nuts to wash their clothing, and these nuts have many qualities but can already alterate the color after four or five washings. Also the biggest issue in India is the lack of public toilets (sorry if you are eating). The result is that you have manure all over the place so that the water is not exactly clean. So what is the point of washing clothes with a super effective cleaning product if the water is a bit filthy?

3.2.4 The Essence of a Substitution Product

Third question, and then I had to stop as I felt I was upsetting the cleaning experts attending: "What type of smell do you plan to develop? How sensitive to smell are your target personas?" They planned to implement the same smell as in Europe as their research concluded there is some kind of universal ideal smell. I did not know so much about smell at that time, but one thing I read is that soap nuts, which belong to the Lychee family, have a neutral smell. In some countries like Switzerland and Germany, people even use them to clean their pets so that they do not get upset by some chemical scent (Ecolana 2008).

The smell revealed to be critical. That was right on time to start looking in a better direction.

3.3 Passing Consumers' Smell Test

Let us explore the world of inhalation and smell, and understand why some brands, like *Häagen Dazs* pass consumers' smell test and others do not.

3.3.1 The Secrets of Smell Perception

3.3.1.1 Inhalation and Smell

Smell can take two pathways: through our nose, or through our throat; for instance when we chew food. Smell is captured by the mucus of the olfactory membrane and detected by the olfactory cilia covering it. The cilia are connected to olfactory sensory neurons, which specialize in groups of odorants. The neurons turn the stimuli into an electric impulse sent to the brain.

Fig. 3.2 Olfactory membrane and smell perception (printed with DervalResearch permission)

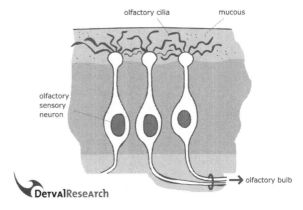

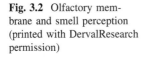

Olfactory cilia are highly exposed, and they regenerate therefore every 30 to 60 days (Fig. 3.2).

Alert signals like gas are directly captured by our sense of danger informants, our nerve endings. In a manner similar to taste, odorants like menthol, ammonia, or chili pepper are perceived by pain receptors (National Institute of Health 2009).

Smelling consists in converting an odorant into neural information. It involves olfactory receptors but also some sniffing power. People suffering from Parkinson's disease for instance are often diagnosed with anosmia, a loss of the ability to smell. A team of researchers decided to 'check if the PC was connected', here if the nose was doing its job, and found out that those patients might in fact have a sniffing impairment: the primary motor component of olfaction that consists in detecting the odorant was not working properly (Sobel et al. 2000).

Humans can distinguish up to 10,000 odors, thanks to 1,000 distinct odorant receptors. Progress has been done recently in that field of research but still *nobody nose* how smell exactly works.

3.3.1.2 Odor, Odorants, and Pheromones

Odorants are components such as dibutylamine that are captured by our mucus; whereas odor is the scent we perceive—here it is likely to be fishy (Iowa State University 2004). To give you an idea, and as we will study in detail later, the odor of an orange is produced by over 300 odorants.

Today's perfumes are often made with synthesized odorants, commonly called *chemical odorants*. Most of them are derived from petroleum, and can trigger allergic reactions. The case is serious and in Canada, for instance, a scent-free policy has been launched in offices as 40% of Canadian suffer from respiratory disease (Canadian Centre for Occupational Health and Safety 2008). Woman were revealed to be four times more sensitive to synthesized odorants than men.

Chemical odorants are present in incense, shampoos, sunscreen, and cleaning products. So using soap nuts is not that silly after all.

Did You Know? Elizabeth Taylor, Allergic To Her Own Smell
   Cleopatra was burning incense throughout the day. Ironically, she was incarnated in Hollywood by Elizabeth Taylor, who is also famous for being asthmatic. In 1991, the actress created her own fragrance "White Diamonds", named after her passion for jewellery. The perfume is a classic with Lily and Aldehyde notes (Osmoz). Aldehyde is a bitter and fatty plant (pungent) that, in the same way as smoke and chlorine, triggers asthma (Caceres et al. 2009). Elizabeth, if you read this book, change perfume!

We sense odorants but also pheromones. This non verbal language is used to alert, attract, or scare away our peers. Ants, for instance, use this volatile stimulus to communicate the food direction to their colleagues. Certain species even mark with a repellent pheromone the roads not leading to food anymore—like a 'road closed' sign (Jeanson et al. 2003).

3.3.1.3 Chemical Sensitivity

Further investigation on sense of smell confirms that 16 to 33% of a given population presents chemical sensitivity to not only cleaning agents, but also to perfumes and flower scents. The symptoms reported include: coughing, blocked nose, heavy breathing, and pressure on the chest.

Capsaicin, an active component of chili peppers, is helpful in diagnosing people suffering from this "airway sensory hyper-reactivity" (SHR): 80% of the people who reported odor intolerances reacted positively to capsaicin by coughing 35 times in the 10 min following inhalation of capsaicin nebulized with a concentration of 2.0 µmol/L. Not a very nice way of checking, but at least it is measurable (Johansson et al. 2006).

If we make a parallel with the Maslow Pyramid of needs, we could say that air, food, and mate odorants are key for survival, whereas floral and alcohol odorants are less needed. We could probably also live without chemical and toxic odorants. Interestingly, consumers present different sensory profiles regarding smell that seem linked to these priorities (Fig. 3.3).

3.3.1.4 Inhaler Profiles

Age, gender, and also ethnicity have an influence on the perception of smell.

In research conducted on 1,198 subjects exposed to 50 odorants, men were on average slightly better than women in recognizing peanut, onion, chocolate, watermelon, banana, and cheddar. Women clearly overperformed men on coconut, dill, lime, gingerbread, cedar, musk, and black pepper. Women had on average a better detection and recognition of smell than men: they not only can better sense the presence of an odorant, but can also name it. Variation in women's performance was noted during pregnancy and menstruation (Doty and Cameron 2009).

Fig. 3.3 Derval Pyramid of
scents sensitivity (printed
with DervalResearch
permission)

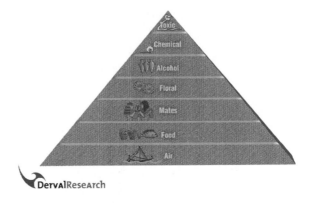

Fig. 3.4 Inhaler profiles
(printed with DervalResearch
permission)

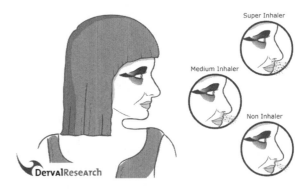

Individuals have a very different perception of smell, not only in terms of intensity but also in terms of pleasantness. Some are more sensitive to chemicals. Based on previous research and our own observations, we segmented consumers according to their inhaler profile into three groups: non-inhalers, medium-inhalers and super-inhalers (Fig. 3.4).

Super-inhalers, mainly women, are very sensitive to chemicals and prefer food to floral scents. Medium-inhalers enjoy food and subtle floral notes, such as rose. Non-inhalers, mainly men, are less sensitive to chemicals, and appreciate spicy or musky notes (Table 3.1).

Elizabeth Taylor, an asthmatic, would clearly be a super-inhaler and Cleopatra, burning incense, a non-inhaler.

These profiles can help you identify your target consumers and develop the right sensory mix.

During clinical testing performed in the US, 20.8% of the women in their 70s reported smell impairments, against 40.6% for age-matched men. Age limits smell ability but the differences observed between genders remain (Table 3.2).

Strong disparities also exist among people of the same gender. A study compared the perception of 40 Japanese and 44 age-matched German women exposed to 18 odorants including French anise spirit *Ricard*, blue cheese, the

Table 3.1 Scent preferences by inhaler profile

	Non-inhaler	Medium-inhaler	Super-inhaler
Food	Appreciate spicy notes, chocolate, peppermint, and lemon. Does not like fishy odors	Prefers baking bread, vanilla, or coffee. Does not like fishy odors	Prefers vanilla, and orange notes, or steak smell
Mates	Likes musky notes	Sensitive to musky notes	Very sensitive to musky odors
Baby powder	Does not identify easily	Perceives as floral	Perceives as sweet
Floral	Enjoys lilacs, lavender, and wooden notes	Likes jasmine, fresh grass, and rose. Does not like sewer or garbage odor	Floral scents are irritating
Alcohol	Likes the smell of alcohol and sometimes petroleum	Does not mind alcohol smell	Perceives alcohol smell as irritating
Chemical	Less sensitive to chemicals	Can find some chemicals, and cigarette smoke irritating	Very sensitive to chemicals, and cigarette smoke
Population	25%, mainly men	50%	25%, mainly women
Capsaicin test	Few coughs	15 coughs	35 coughs

Based on 1,200 observations and measurements conducted by DervalResearch between May 2009 and February 2010 in over 25 countries

Table 3.2 Smell impairments in elderly (National Institute of Health 2009)

Age	Women (%)	Men (%)
53–59	3.8	9.1
60–69	11.2	24.7
70–79	20.8	40.6
80–97	59.4	69.5

Proportion detected among subjects during clinical testings in the US

Table 3.3 Top 3 intense odorants for Japanese and German women

Odorants intensity	Japanese	German
No. 1	Perfume	Dried fish
No. 2	Coffee	Menthol
No. 3	Incense	Coffee

Source: Ayabe-Kanamura et al. (1998)

Table 3.4 Top 3 favorite odorants for Japanese and German women

Favorite odorants	Japanese	German
No. 1	Coffee	Coffee
No. 2	Peanuts	Perfume
No. 3	Chocolate	Chocolate

Source: Ayabe-Kanamura et al. (1998)

perfume *Angel*, coffee, chocolate, peanuts, dried fish, menthol, incense, and salami (Ayabe-Kanamura et al. 1998).

The first observation was that they did not perceive a same odorant as having the same intensity. Japanese women perceived perfume (containing alcohol) and incense as very intense, whereas German women perceived dried fish and menthol as more intense. Coffee was considered in the top three of the most intense smell by both groups. For both groups, almonds and pine wood were the least intense smells (Table 3.3).

In terms of preferences, coffee and chocolate were in the top three of both groups. Japanese women also ranked peanuts as a favorite odorant, German women preferred perfume (Table 3.4).

In terms of worst smell, both groups were unanimous about soybeans and blue cheese (how is this possible, tasty French cheese? I am shocked). German women did not appreciate the smell of Japanese Houjicha tea, a roasted tea that smells of something burnt. Japanese women disliked most the church incense. Incense, like for instance, olibanum, is an aromatic resin from trees, rich in terpenes, with a spicy/lemon type of smell. While burning, incense also produces smoke (Table 3.5).

Based on this research, Japanese women are more sensitive to alcohol and chemicals like incense, than German women, and could be considered as super-

Table 3.5 Top 3 worst odorants for Japanese and German Women

Worst odorants	Japanese	German
No. 1	Incense	Soybeans
No. 2	Blue cheese	Blue cheese
No. 3	Soybeans	Japanese tea

Source: Ayabe-Kanamura et al. (1998)

inhalers. German women perceive strongly odorants like menthol, stimulating the temperature and pain receptors, but enjoy at the same time perfume with alcohol, and could therefore be considered as medium inhalers.

Odorants can be pleasant or irritating and can also be powerful endocrine disruptors, triggering different hormonal reactions, and influencing our mood and behavior.

3.3.1.5 Ambient Odorants and Mood

In aromatherapy, essential oils like lavender or rosemary are used for their sedative or stimulating properties (Carr and Carr 2003). Some of them are natural and do not include petrochemical residues. However, many oils are produced by distillation and include alcohol.

Sedative essential oils include lavender and cedarwood. Lavender oil is involved in the secretion of cyclic adenosine monophosphate (cAMP), which regulates the effects of adrenaline—similarly to cannabis. And this calming effect can be very useful in stressful contexts like the dentist waiting room! Both men and women exposed to orange and lavender essential oils were more relaxed and in a better mood. Ambient odors were even more effective than music in making waiting subjects feel less anxious. Note that the selected tune "Cafe' del Mar— Music from Ibiza" was probably not suited to all ears, as we learned in Chap. 2 (Lehrner et al. 2005).

On the other hand, stimulating essential oils like rosemary enhance our productivity. In an experiment, people were exposed to lavender or to rosemary essential oils, or to nothing, and then asked to perform different tasks like calculations, image recognition, and simple decision making. The speed and quality of attention and memory were measured on the three groups. Compared to the control group, both lavender and rosemary groups declared feeling more relaxed. Subjects exposed to lavender were the least effective in task completion whereas subjects exposed to rosemary were outperforming the others, including the control group not exposed to the essential oils. Interestingly, lavender impaired the working memory, the equivalent of a computer Random Access Memory (RAM), in charge of encoding, storing and retrieving information, and rosemary enhanced the secondary memory, the equivalent of a computer Read Only Memory (ROM), in charge of storing and organizing the data on the long term (Moss et al. 2003).

So basically, if you want consumers to remember all the good reasons why they should buy your new product so that they have enough arguments to convince their spouse when they are back home, do not expose them to lavender. Also, if your invoice is a bit expensive, make sure customers do not smell rosemary while they pay, otherwise they might remember this painful experience forever.

3.3.1.6 A Juicy Story

When you have a look at the composition of essential oils, you see many things except what you would expect. A gas chromatography, technique that enables you to isolate all the volatiles present in an odor, revealed in previous research that main components of the orange essential oil used, in the brand Primavera, are limonene at 95.3% and myrcene at 1.88%, all other components being below 1%. Limonene is an irritating terpene used in paints, cleaning products, and botanical insecticides. It can be found in small quantities in orange peels.

What happened to the orange? I mean the real oranges?

In my desperate quest for freshly squeezed oranges in cafes and restaurants, I realized that the business ethics of some owners is doubtful—freshly squeezed often means freshly coming out of a bottle. Of course some artifices used, like fake added pulp, might give the juice the appearance of fresh juice. Luckily my tongue full of taste buds always discovers the truth. When confronted, the business owner's lie on the juice's origin would be expressed with such conviction that I often truly believed he/she just did not taste the difference—a typical taster versus non-taster misunderstanding, as demonstrated in Chap. 1.

What I realized is that not only the taste but also the smell was helping me detect the pretender. I am talking about the juice, of course. Note that pheromones might at the same time indicate to me that the owner was lying. The over 300 odorants of orange juice can be altered in many ways: through the extraction and preservation process, pulp separation, and packaging. Some odorants disappear and others appear (Perez-Cacho and Rouseff 2005). Just having the same orange squeezed mechanically instead of manually makes a huge difference, as the machine includes more peel. In mechanically squeezed orange juice, you will find:

- Three to ten times more limonene, our irritating terpene friend.
- Ten to 45 times more aldehydes, our asthma triggering friend.

The type of orange is also critical: the Tarocco, a variety of blood oranges, contains less limonene than other examined oranges like *Moro* or *Valencia Late*.

So, if you are a super inhaler, not only should you drink freshly squeezed blood oranges, but you should make sure they are squeezed manually. By the way, check that they were not exposed to pesticides; because remember, pesticides can contain limonene, too.

Using ambient odors is a great opportunity to influence your consumers' mood. Just keep in mind that all kind of odorants are present in nature but in nano quantities. The issue with non natural and processed products is that they concentrate odorants at irritating levels.

Let us see how smell can enhance other senses in a subtle way with the *Sofitel Amsterdam The Grand* Carousel of Senses case.

3.3.2 Sofitel Amsterdam The Grand *Carousel of Senses*

The Grand, a former monastery, has since 1578 been accommodating royalty. Not only the queen but also the parents of the General Manager, Robert-Jan Woltering, got married in this five stars de luxe hotel. Robert-Jan has a food and beverage background, and opened Sofitel resorts in Dubai, Egypt, and Luxembourg.

When he joined *Sofitel Amsterdam The Grand*, two things bothered him: (1) The hotel was not predominant in the press and in the city, (2) people of Amsterdam were not coming here anymore. With its new sensory strategy, The Grand is back on the map! The hotel, a piece of 'French Elegance in the Dutch Cultural Heritage', welcomes international dignitaries and also pop stars such as Robbie Williams, and Beyoncé (Woltering 2010).

The idea of The Grand re-opening, celebrated in September 2010, was to position the hotel as a super luxury hotel and to propose different atmospheres: more futuristic at the bar, more classical in the Council Chamber, relaxing with the SoSpa, and sportive with the SoFit center.

French architect Sybille de Margerie, who also re-designed Parisian Hôtel de Crillon, created with the help of five students from the Design Academy in Eindhoven, 112 specific room atmospheres, each one around a unique piece of art, with new concepts like a "salle de bien"—literally a well-being bathroom. For the restaurant, she was inspired by Karel Appel's mural displayed in the restaurant area, and proposed an unusual and vibrant palette of colors (Fig. 3.5). At delivery in 1949, when The Grand was serving as Amsterdam cityhall, the civil servants covered the painting as many visitors of the cantina reported losing their appetite when seeing its disturbing colors, or was it maybe because of its topic 'vragende kinderen' (or 'asking children'), which refers to post-war German children begging for food? The architect brought the painting back into the picture and built a bridge in front of it using natural textures like mahogany, marble and steel. It gave its name to the restaurant—The Bridge's. The restaurant is full since a reputable but feared local critic—the Anton Ego from Pixar's Ratatouille—gave a ten out of ten to the Dutch fish specialties prepared with a French twist by Chef Aurélien Poirot.

Together with top chefs and oenologists, *The Grand* decided to stimulate the senses of their guests, coming from around the globe and especially the US, UK, Germany, and the Middle-East, with *The Grand Carousel of Senses*. Local happy fews including Harold Goddijn, CEO of TomTom, were also invited.

While taste buds are enjoying fine food and wines, inner-ear hair cells vibrate along with music composed to accompany each meal, and olfactory cilia catch the

Fig. 3.5 Sofitel Amsterdam The Grand (printed with permission)

scents sent by a DJ Fragrances, sometimes amplifying sometimes complementing the meal! The meals illustrate five moods: sensual, audacious, extravagant, serene, and nostalgic. Sensual like oysters with a glass of Champagne Gosset, oldest Champagne maison, since 1584. Audacious like a shrimp cocktail, extravagant like a cabillaud, serene like a foie gras, or nostalgic like an apple pie.

This festival is part of the *Stars, Food & Art* initiative and gathered together 12 chefs, and a total of 29 Michelin stars. Robert-Jan Woltering is now the Ambassador of this concept within Sofitel, and Munich, Rabat, New-York, and Abu-Dhabi are the next destinations of this sensory festival.

Associating meals with natural fragrances enhances non-tasters' experience, as their ability to taste is limited, without irritating super-inhalers. Being nose-friendly is very possible and requires just a bit of quality. Häagen Dazs offers another example of successful sensory mix.

3.3.3 A Popular Scent: Häagen Dazs Vanilla Ice-Cream

Our smell system involves olfactory and somatosensory (touch, temperature, proprioception, and pain) reactions. The vast majority of chemosensory stimulants produce both odor and irritation. A research study conducted on anosmic patients, showed that they were surprisingly able to detect 45 out of the 47 tested odorants, such as menthol, as most of them stimulate in fact the temperature and pain receptors. The two undetected odorants were decanoic acid, which occurs in coconut oil and milk, and vanillin (Doty et al. 1978). Vanillin is now known as being a purely olfactive odorant, not causing irritation. This does not mean that everybody likes vanilla, but the risks of sensitive reactions after inhalation of this odorant are limited. A popular but expensive spice native to Mexico, vanilla gives its aroma to liqueurs, perfumes, cigars, and ice-creams (Encyclopedia of species 2003).

Who would have thought an entrepreneur from the Bronx would build a vanilla empire? Starting with three ice-cream flavors (coffee, chocolate, and vanilla) in 1920, Häagen-Dazs is now available in 54 countries, with flavor going from Mint to Lemon. Guess what: their best-selling flavor is by far vanilla (Häagen-Dazs 2005). Their new campaign highlights the fact that their sensory mix includes only five ingredients: milk, cream, sugar, eggs, and of course, vanilla (Fig. 3.6).

The sensory evaluation with notes of dairy complex, cooked and butter fat, eggy aromas, and vanilla impressions, including vanillin, bourbon/alcohol, and dried fruit odors, confirms that what you smell is what you get.

Now part of the Nestlé group, the brand is challenged by the increase in cost for its fine ingredients such as vanilla from Madagascar and decided to shrink the quantity in a carton from 470 to 410 ml instead of sacrificing the quality. Our smell and taste receptors appreciate this move. A recent campaign orchestrated by the premium ice-cream leader, with 45% market-share, for saving bees from extinction helped raise considerable attention and funds for research. Häagen-Dazs is truly motivated as their precious ingredient vanilla is pollinated by bees, the only creatures capable of penetrating the tough vanilla membrane!

Fig. 3.6 Häagen Dazs
vanilla ice-cream aromatics
(Melligard et al. 2007)

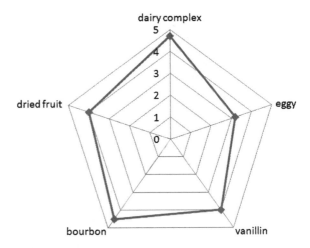

So vanilla is popular because it does not attack our nose. Let us see if we can explain other scent preferences.

3.3.4 Predicting Scents Preferences

As sensitivity to smell and chemicals is linked to gender, age, ethnicity, and hormonal variation, I started retroducting again. Having in mind our previous study on taste and sound, I wondered if our scent preferences were also linked to hormones and therefore predictable.

We conducted a research study together with St. Croix Sensory Inc., a company applying clinical tools to the environmental industry and training odor inspectors with cutting edge ambient odor testing tools such as the Nasal Ranger. They help governments, industries, and citizen groups assess odors. Their panel of 50 trained assessors, all women, even outperformed the smell ability of the field inspectors of the US Environmental Protection Agency, mainly men!

We selected 23 women between 50 and 69 years old. We asked them to list their favorite and worst smell (Table 3.6).

We grouped the favorite smells in three categories:

- Food: steak, vanilla, apple, baked bread, chinese food, ginger, cinnamon, orange.
- Flower: lilacs, clean linen, jasmine, flowers.
- Food/flower: a special category for baby powder, alternatively perceived as 'food' (sweet) or 'flower' (rose), depending on the individual (Lawless 1999).

This intriguing baby powder case calls for further research. Super-tasters sense sugar as being two to four times sweeter, maybe super-inhalers also sense a sweet smell more intensely. In the same way, some like the smell of petroleum. They are probably less sensitive to alcohol, in a similar manner to the non-tasters. This would support recent conclusions that hormones maintain similar functions in

Table 3.6 Favorite, worst smell, and digit ratio in 23 women aged 50–69

ID	Gender	Age	Favorite smell	Worst smell	Digit ratio	Prenatal hormones
S1	F	50–54	Flower	Organic	1.000	Estrogen-driven
S2	F	50–54	Flower	Organic	0.971	Testosterone-driven
S3	F	55–59	Food	Organic	0.985	Testosterone-driven
S4	F	55–59	Flower	Organic	1.046	Estrogen-driven
S5	F	55–59	Flower	Organic	1.075	Estrogen-driven
S6	F	55–59	Food	Organic	0.957	Testosterone-driven
S7	F	55–59	Food	Organic	0.985	Testosterone-driven
S8	F	55–59	Food	Organic	0.986	Testosterone-driven
S9	F	55–59	Food	Organic	0.944	Testosterone-driven
S10	F	60–64	Food/Flower	Chemical	0.886	Testosterone-driven
S11	F	60–64	Food	Organic	1.057	Estrogen-driven
S12	F	60–64	Food	Chemical	0.897	Testosterone-driven
S13	F	60–64	Food	Chemical	1.029	Estrogen-driven
S14	F	60–64	Food/Flower	Organic	0.986	Testosterone-driven
S15	F	60–64	Flower	Organic	0.961	Testosterone-driven
S16	F	60–64	Food	Chemical	0.987	Testosterone-driven
S17	F	60–64	Air	Organic	0.959	Testosterone-driven
S18	F	60–64	Flower	Organic	1.029	Estrogen-driven
S19	F	60–64	Flower	Organic	1.014	Estrogen-driven
S20	F	60–64	Food	Chemical	0.959	Testosterone-driven
S21	F	65–69	Food	Organic	1.000	Estrogen-driven
S22	F	65–69	Flower	Organic	1.015	Estrogen-driven
S23	F	65–69	Food	Chemical	1.000	Estrogen-driven

Research conducted by DervalResearch with the collaboration of St. Croix Sensory Inc. in January 2010 (Derval 2010)

different organs and parts of the metabolism, ensuring a certain consistency of the sensorial system (Martin et al. 2009). I just received bottles of baby powder and will have them sniffed for my next research study!

We grouped the worst smell into two categories:

- Organic: garbage, vomit, eggs, septic, sewer, urine, dish, necrotic, burnt food, skunk.
- Chemical: petroleum, cleaning products, ammonia, cigarette, chemicals, chlorine.

We measured the influence of prenatal hormones on each assessor with the digit ratio, a non-invasive technique based on anthropomorphic measurements, which we will explore in detail later in this chapter. Women with a digit ratio >1.00 are estrogen-driven ($n = 10$), with a digit ratio <1.00 they are testosterone-driven ($n = 13$). The separation is marked by a line on the chart (Fig. 3.7).

When introducing this hormonal segmentation criteria, suddenly the data formed two homogeneous groups: 'food' women, testosterone-driven, and 'flower' women, estrogen-driven. Now I understand why I always preferred a box of chocolates to a bunch of flowers!

Indeed, the outcome is:

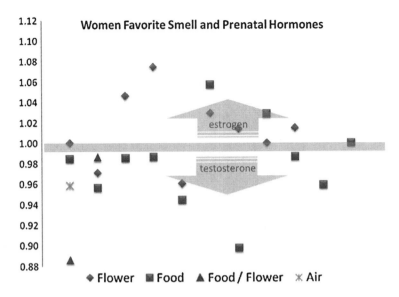

Fig. 3.7 Women favorite smell and prenatal hormones (Derval 2010)

- Among the nine women who prefer a flower smell, seven are estrogen-driven and two are testosterone-driven.
- Among the 11 women who prefer a food smell, eight are testosterone-driven and three are estrogen-driven.

Among the six women sensitive to chemicals, four were testosterone-driven (Fig. 3.8). That could point out that sensitivity to chemicals is linked to prenatal exposure to testosterone in women, possibly weakening the immune system. These findings were presented at the 14th Annual Meeting of the Society for Behavioral Neuroendocrinology in Toronto.

Looking at these two groups of 'flower' and 'food' women, I was thinking that gender segmentation could after all be very accurate, with more than two genders! I was suddenly eager to learn more about genetics, hormones, and genders.

3.4 Male, Female, and Chicken

We see how genes and hormones can influence gender, traits, and behavior in chickens, lizards, but also in humans, and from an early age. Analyzing the differences between innate and acquired traits and behaviors will reveal the predicting power of hormones.

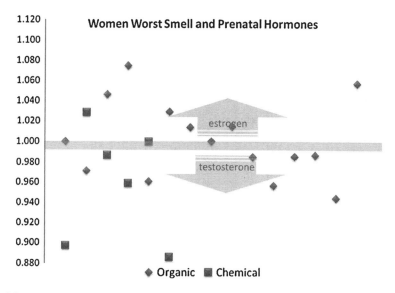

Fig. 3.8 Women worst smell and prenatal hormones (Derval 2010)

3.4.1 Genetics and Hormones

Many animal species, including birds, fishes, and lizards, count more than two genders. I am not talking here about drag-chickens, but about different expressions of male and female, called gender polymorphism. These multiple genders were easily detected in some species where each group has a distinctive appearance—often it is the color.

The ultimate of the number of genders among animals comes to the side-blotched lizard, with three male and two female genders (Alonzo and Sinervo 2001):

- Orange-throated males, aggressive, with high level of testosterone, and dating several females.
- Blue-throated males, less testosterone, less aggressive, taking care of one female at a time.
- Yellow-throated males, with no fixed territory.
- Orange-throated females, laying many eggs (5.9 per batch), distant to other females.
- Yellow-throated females, laying fewer but bigger eggs (5.6 per batch), more tolerant with other females.

The polymorphism is not limited to the appearance but concerns also the physical traits and the behavior of the individuals, and is directly linked to prenatal hormones. Among *Urosaurus ornatus* tree lizards for instance, there are two male genders:

- Orange-blue males are small and very aggressive.
- Orange males are longer and less aggressive, and they are not fixed to a territory.

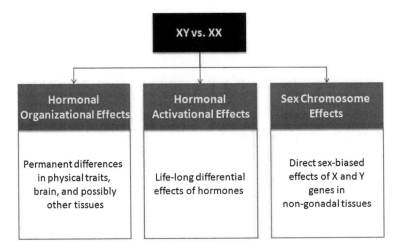

Fig. 3.9 XY versus XX: three expressions of sex differences (Arnold et al. 2009)

By injecting progesterone the day a lizard hatches from the egg, researchers can make sure he turns into an orange-blue male.

The theory is that X and Y genes influence gender expression directly via sex chromosome effects, but also indirectly via hormonal effects. These hormonal effects can be 'organizational' or 'activational' (Arnold et al. 2009) (Fig. 3.9).

In the example of our tree lizards, the action of prenatal hormones 'organized' his body and brain. This is why the lizard turns into an orange-blue male after exposure to progesterone. Other behaviors are 'activated' like when orange males have an increase in corticosterone due to the stress of being thirsty and decide to become nomadic to seek for food and beverages whereas orange-blue lizard never perceive similar stress signals (Roughgarden 2004).

These combined effects of genetics and hormones are also observed in humans and explain for instance the differences in incidence and progression of diseases. We will also see later that 'the organizational effects' of hormones on other tissues concern our sensory receptors.

3.4.2 Women are from Mars and Men from Venus

Understanding differences helps de-dramatize situations. So learning about differences in communications between men and women from the book *Men are from Mars, Women are from Venus*, probably saved many weddings (Gray 1993).

The examples given are often from the dominant gender polymorphism. And it is true that most of the studies are busy with the influence of testosterone on men. The influence of testosterone on women and the influence of estrogen on men have been less documented. What about women from Mars and men from Venus? Luckily, some researchers spent time observing lizards and birdies.

White-throated sparrows have males and females with a white stripe, more aggressive, and males and females with a pan stripe, more care-taking. Opposites apparently attract to form the best teams, capable of both protection and nurturing, as 90% of the couples are white-striped males with pan-striped females or white-striped females with pan-striped males (Roughgarden 2004). Important to note is that, like in humans, hormones can have an influence on behavior without having any impact on sexual preferences.

3.4.3 Innate Versus Acquired

In humans, the 'organizational effects' of prenatal testosterone and estrogen set our physical and personality traits while we are still a fetus, and this is independent of our gender (Pinel 2007). We already know before the 14th week if we will have generous breasts or be bald (Manning 2002).

The 'activational effects' of prenatal hormones have been less clearly identified, as behavior and preferences are often attributed to psychological or cultural factors, without further retroduction. The more I observe people and know about lizards, the more I see similarities! Let us see why people exposed to the same prenatal hormones behave similarly.

3.4.3.1 Prenatal Hormones, Vocation, and Hobbies

The impact of testosterone on physical and sports abilities has been demonstrated—it quickens the recovery from muscular activities. The doping industry has already jumped on this opportunity and is widely using steroids to boost results (Pinel 2007). Testosterone seems also to be a driver in male:male competition and the willingness to dominate (Manning 2002).

The impact of testosterone and estrogen on sensation seeking has also been demonstrated. High sensation seekers tend to go for scientific, artistic, or social careers, becoming for instance a social worker, or a researcher (Zuckerman 1994).

Individuals can express their sensation seeking in different ways (Zuckerman 1994). Men get involved in illegal car races or extreme sports, like our Red Bull drinkers. In fact, they do not perceive those activities as risky and their nervous system does not even generate the related fear, anxiety, or stress signals—a bit like orange-blue lizards (Roberti 2004).

3.4.3.2 Prenatal Hormones, and Sensory Perception

The exposure to prenatal testosterone and estrogen has a great influence on our physical and personality traits, but also on our sensory perception.

Women entrepreneurs, for instance, are very testosterone-driven, or very estrogen-driven, and are mainly super-tasters. On the other hand, women nurses are equally influenced by both prenatal hormones and are mainly non-tasters (Derval 2009). As nurses report less chronic diseases than women entrepreneurs, who are more subject to allergies and other disorders, it is well possible that the number of taste buds is adapted to the level of protection needed by the body—their primary function is to alert us on toxic food. This would explain why extreme sports fans are also poorer in taste buds and more likely to enjoy Red Bull.

Hormonally balanced individuals are from our observations more involved in team activities, report a stronger immune system, and less sensitivities. This was the case in our 'flower' versus 'food' segmentation, where testosterone-driven women were more sensitive to chemicals. If we go back to our research on sound perception and check the link between prenatal hormones and the hearing sensitivity of our 16 men in their 30s, we will find the following:

- Non-amplifiers ($n = 4$) are hormonally balanced and report no particular sensitivity to loudness.
- Super-amplifiers ($n = 4$) are testosterone-driven or estrogen-driven and report being sensitive to high-pitched noise (mosquito, baby, klaxon) (Derval 2010b).

As we will see in following chapters, the 'organizational effects' of hormones on sensory perception are also verified with touch and vision.

3.4.3.3 Measuring Prenatal Hormones

Among the several ways of measuring prenatal hormones, the digit ratio technique is the least invasive. We used it in our different studies. Here is how it works.

The ratio between the index and ring finger is determined when we are a fetus and remains the same. It is considered as a reliable biological marker of the 'organizational effects' of hormones. Our digit ratio or hormonal fingerprint can be measured by comparing the length between the index and the ring finger on the right hand: a shorter index is a sign of higher exposure to prenatal testosterone (Manning 2002) (Fig. 3.10). You can check your hormonal fingerprint with the ruler.

The average digit ratio for Caucasian women is 1.00, which means that both fingers have the same length. For Caucasian men the index is a bit shorter with an average ratio of 0.98. Strong disparities were measured in different countries with an average digit ratio for men of 0.97 in Hungary and of 0.93 in Jamaica or a digit ratio of 0.99 for women in Spain and 0.97 in India (Table 3.7).

> Did You Know? Digit Ratio and Forensics
> Indian Forensics, the scientific investigation unit, uses the digit ratio technique to identify the gender of isolated hands. They tested the method on 150 men and 150 women. 80% of the measured Indian men presented a digit ratio < 0.97 and 78% of the measured Indian women presented a ratio > 0.97 (Kanchana et al. 2008). So, if my calculations are accurate, 20% of Indian men are from Venus and 22% of Indian women are from Mars.

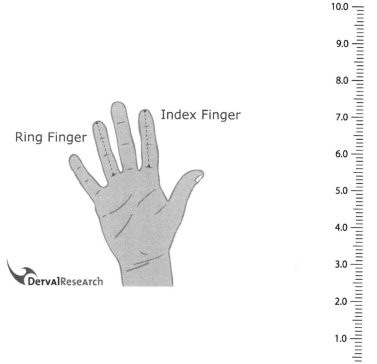

Fig. 3.10 Digit ratio or Hormonal Fingerprint (printed with DervalResearch permission)

Average digit ratio	Men	Women
Poland	0.99	1.00
Spain	0.99	0.99
England	0.98	0.99
Hungary	0.97	0.98
Germany	0.96	0.97
India	0.96	0.97
Finland	0.94	0.96
Jamaica	0.93	0.94

Table 3.7 Average digit ratio per Country (Manning 2002)

3.4.4 Toy Story

Measuring the influence of prenatal hormones at an early stage can help prevent diseases, manage sensory sensitivities, and propose adapted activities to each child. Did I tell you about my *Playmobil* trauma?

This is a perfect example of wrong marketing segmentation. I was around 5, coming from Mars, and at school we were celebrating Christmas. I could not believe my eyes when I saw this mountain of *Playmobil* castles in the class room and was heading in their direction to grab my box when the teacher, a bit surprised, poked me and showed me where my gift actually was: she pointed in direction of another table full of baby-dolls. What was I supposed to do with a baby-doll?

I have partly recovered and since then I regularly play with LEGO® to catch up.

Luckily with current knowledge in behavioral neuroendocrinology, we are able to define sharper marketing segments, and propose the right sensory mix to our clients, as we will see right now with the Hormonal Quotient™ (HQ).

3.5 Targeting Consumers with the Hormonal Quotient™ (HQ)

Even if the limits of the 'one-size-fits-all' approach sound obvious, I cannot resist sharing some anecdotes with you. They will urge the need for a consumer segmentation based on sensors. We will see how consumers are at the same time unique and predictable, and analyze the benefits of predictive segmentation tools for delivering multisensory experiences.

3.5.1 Limits of the 'One-Size-Fits-All' Approach

As we saw previously, there is no ideal taste, music, or smell. Making sure that the stimuli is not irritating our consumers could be a good start. Here are some nice examples of sensory non-senses.

A restaurant celebrated its re-opening after a complete make-over. The menu promised fine foods and expensive Champagne. But a fresh paint smell caused a few people to feel nauseous and they left the party as soon as they could because of the chemical attack. Among them, the journalist in charge of covering the event, a super-inhaler.

The call center of a consumer electronics brand of food mixers received several complaints from consumers about a plastic taste in their juice (and as seen previously, it is difficult enough to get a good juice). As only a couple of people reported the issue, it was not taken seriously. Unfortunately, the concerned consumers were mainly Chris persona, our trendsetter medium-taster, so that soon all the details about the incident and its bad management were available in many Internet forums.

A fine French cheese shop, famous for its delicatessen and for attracting a crowd of gourmets and French expats, decided to cut some peripheral costs and to wrap up the cheese with a cheaper plastic film. Bad idea, as some consumers, super inhalers and respected connoisseurs, immediately detected the chemical smell when unwrapping their precious cheese. They stopped promoting the shop.

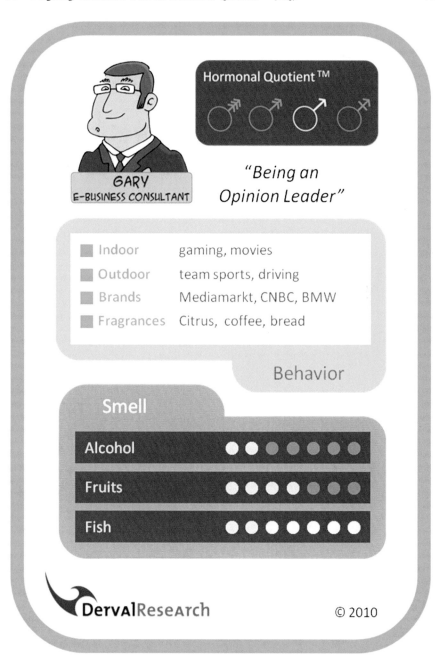

Fig. 3.11 Hormonal Quotient™ (HQ) of Gary (printed with DervalResearch permission)

Fig. 3.12 Gender, prenatal hormones, organizational effects, and Hormonal Quotient™ (HQ)

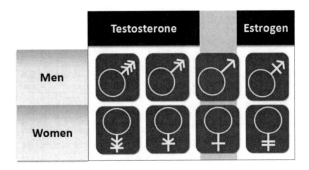

It is well worth identifying the sensory sensitivities of your target consumers before applying some "on-size-fits-all" rules and delivering a disastrous service or product to your most precious clients.

3.5.2 Sensors and Segmentation

The best way to assess the sensory perception of consumers is to observe them.

Gary, a successful e-business consultant, just bought a new BMW and plans to give his rugby friends a ride after work. He is bothered by the mix of crayon and leather smell of the freshly bought car and runs into a car accessories shop. He tells his story to the vendor, who proposes an odor neutralizer with a citrus smell. Gary loves the fragrance and leaves the shop happy. What happened?

When Gary entered the shop, the vendor immediately knew based on Gary's gender, age, appearance, job, and hobbies, that this consumer was a medium inhaler and that therefore his favorite smells are baked bread, coffee, and citrus (Fig. 3.11). He also read in the news that baked bread smell was not recommended for drivers because it makes them feel hungry and increases the risk of excessive speed and car rages (Bakeryandsnacks.com 2005). And as his coffee odor neutralizer was out, he automatically handed out the citrus one.

This is not science fiction, it is sensory segmentation. And it works because even if consumers are unique, they are very predictable.

3.5.3 Consumers Are Unique but Predictable!

We saw earlier in this chapter that the 'organizational effects' of hormones influence consumers, physical traits, behavior, job, and hobbies, but also the density and sensitivity of their sensory receptors. This is why extreme sports players and nurses are non-tasters, and why women entrepreneurs are super-tasters. The expression of this influence varies depending on gender, and on ethnicity. Age, menstruation, and pregnancy, and the associated hormonal variations, can also modify the sensory perception.

We called the influence of hormones on our traits, behavior, and sensory perception our Hormonal Quotient™ (HQ). We measured it on thousands of consumers in over 25 countries since 2007 and were able to identify four Hormonal Quotient™ (HQ) for men, and four Hormonal Quotient™ (HQ) for women, depending on the organizational effects of prenatal testosterone and estrogen. Consumers of each group presented similar behavior and sensory responses (Fig. 3.12).

Women can be equally influenced by testosterone and estrogen—they are represented by the standard female symbol we are familiar with—or estrogen-driven (with two stripes instead of one), or on the other side testosterone-driven (with an arrow), or very testosterone-driven (with two arrows).

Men can be equally influenced by testosterone and estrogen—they are represented by the standard male symbol we are familiar with—or testosterone-driven (with two arrows instead of one), or very testosterone-driven (with three arrows), or on the other side estrogen-driven (with a stripe).

With strong variations between countries, we observed that 50% of the men and women are equally influenced by testosterone and estrogen, that 20% of the men and 25% of the women are estrogen-driven, and that 30% of the men and 25% of the women are testosterone-driven.

If you want to assess your Hormonal Quotient™ (HQ), you can take the quick test at http://www.derval-research.com.

3.5.4 Hormonal Quotient™ (HQ) and Multisensory Perception

In the same way that consumer experience is a whole, sensory experience is by definition multisensory as it stimulates several senses at the same time. A cup of coffee will stimulate your taste buds and your olfactive receptors. Music will vibrate in your inner-ear and also under your skin, as you will discover in the next chapter.

Did You Know? In Greek, 'hormone' means 'stimulate'.

A square-shaped coffee machine is more likely to attract testosterone-driven consumers. If the consumer is a testosterone-driven woman, such as Marcia, she is more likely to be sensitive to bitterness and will expect a mild coffee. Her male counterpart is more likely to be a non-taster and will enjoy an espresso. *Nespresso* solved this dilemma by proposing coffee capsules with different strengths and colors. Did you ever wonder why their milder capsules (*Lungo* and *Arpeggio*) are in more vibrant colors? You will enjoy our chapter on vision then.

Also, if we go back to our detergent case in India, local Forensics confirms that 22% of the women are very testosterone-driven and will probably not appreciate a chemical cleaning product with, on top of it, a flower scent.

When collecting, measuring, and documenting over 50 target groups including top executives, housewives, entrepreneurs, purchasing managers, and trendsetters, we got the confirmation that their multisensory perceptions were comparable, and

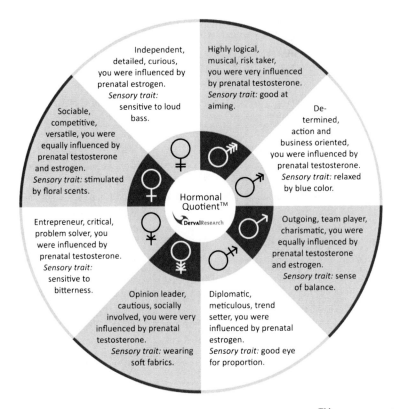

Fig. 3.13 Example of personality and sensory traits by Hormonal Quotient™ (HQ) (printed with DervalResearch permission)

by knowing some individuals with the same Hormonal Quotient™ (HQ), we were able to accurately predict the behavior and preferences of others individuals of the same group, in the same context (Fig. 3.13).

In this chapter, we saw how to use powerful predictive tools in order to segment consumers and predict their main traits and sensory perception.

In next chapter, we will see how, thanks to detailed sensory profiles, you will be able, like our car accessories vendor, to propose the right sensory mix to your customers.

3.6 Take-Aways

Product popularity

- Understanding local usages and habits is key, even in your own country.
- Purchasing intentions are unreliable.
- Substitution products can tell a lot about consumers.

Smell

- Consumers are super, medium or non-inhalers.
- Vanilla is a pure olfactory odorant and is therefore less irritating.
- Testosterone-driven women prefer 'food' scents, estrogen-driven women prefer 'flower' scents.

Gender

- Many species have more than two genders, drag queens excluded.
- Our physical traits and behaviors are influenced by prenatal hormones.
- Our sensory traits are also set by prenatal hormones.

Targeting

- Sensory experience has to be adapted to target consumers.
- Assessing their sensory perception is critical.
- Tools like the Hormonal Quotient^{TM} (HQ) can help segment, target, and predict consumers' behavior and preferences

References

Alonzo SH, Sinervo B (2001) Mate choice games, context-dependent good genes, and genetic cycles in the side-blotched lizard, Uta stansburiana. Behav Ecol Sociobiol 49:176–186

Arnold AP, van Nas A, Lusis AJ (2009) Systems biology asks new question about sex differences. Trends Endocrinol Metab 471–476

Ayabe-Kanamura S, Schicker I, Laska M, Hudson R, Distel H, Kobayakawa T et al (1998) Differences in perception of everyday odors: a Japanese-German Cross-Cultural Study. Chem Senses 23:31–38

Bakeryandsnacks.com (2005) Smell of fresh bread and fast food influences behaviour. From Bakeryandssnacks.com: http://www.Bakeryandsnacks.com/Formulation/Smell-of-fresh-bread-and-fast-food-influences-behaviour. Accessed 12 Mar 2010

Caceres A et al (2009) A sensory neuronalion channel essential for airway inflammation and hyperreactivity in asthma. Proc Natl Acad Sci. doi:10.1073/pnas.0900591106

Canadian Centre for Occupational Health and Safety (2008) Scent-free policy for the workplace. From Canadian Centre for Occupational Health and Safety: http://www.ccohs.ca/oshanswers/hsprograms/scent_free.html. Accessed 14 Mar 2010

Carr C, Carr M (2003) Smell yourself sexy. From BBC: http://www.bbc.co.uk/lancashire/lifestyle/2003/09/16/aromatherapy.shtml. Accessed 12 Mar 2010

Derval D (2010a) Hormonal Fingerprint and smell perception: a segmentation model to understand and predict individuals' scent preferences based on prenatal exposure to hormones. 14th Annual conference of the society for behavioral neuroendocrinology. Society for Behavioral Neuroendocrinology, Toronto

Derval D (2010b) Hormonal Fingerprint and sound perception: a segmentation model to understand and predict individuals 'hearing patterns based on OtoAcoustic Emissons, sensitivity to loudness, and prenatal exposure to hormones. 30th International congress of audiology-ICA 2010. The International Society of Audiology, Sao Paulo

Doty R, Cameron L (2009) Sex differences and reproductive hormone influences on human odor perception. Physiol Behav 97(2):213–228

Doty R et al (1978) Intranasal trigeminal stimulation from odorous volatiles: psychometric responses from anosmic and normal humans. Physiol Behav 20:175–185

Ecolana ch (2008) Wie und wo verwendet man waschnüsse? From Sprechzimmer.ch: http://www.sprechzimmer.ch/sprechzimmer/Marktplatz/Waschnuesse/Wie_und_wo_verwendet_man_Waschnuesse.php. Accessed 27 Feb 2010

Encyclopedia of species (2003) Epicentre: http://www.theepicentre.com/Spices/vanilla.html. Accessed 13 Mar 2010

Gray J (1993) Men are from Mars, women are from Venus. Harper Collins, New York

Häagen-Dazs (2005) The idea for Häagen-Dazs dates back to the early 1920's. From Häagen-Dazs: http://www.nestle.ca/haagen_dazs/en/Company/history/index. Accessed 13 Mar 2010

Iowa State University (2004) The science of smell. Iowa

Jeanson R, Ratnieks F, Deneubourg F (2003) Pheromone trail decay rates on diggerent substrates in the Pharaoh's ant, Monomorium pharaonis. Physiol Entomol 28:192–198

Johansson Å, Millqvist E, Nordin S, Bende M (2006) Relationship between self-reported odor intolerance and sensitivity to inhaled capsaicin. Off Public Am Coll Chest Phys 129:1623–1628

Kanchana TK, Kumarb P, Menezesa R (2008) Index and ring finger ratio—a new sex determinant in south Indian population. Forensic Sci Int 181:53.e1–e4

Lawless H (1999) Descriptive analysis of complex odors: reality, model or illusion? Food Qual Preference 10(4–5):325–332

Lehner J, Marwinski G, Lehr S, Johren P, Deeke L (2005) Ambient odors of orange and lavender reduce anxiety and improve mood in a dental office. Physiol Behav 86(1–2):92–95

Manning JT (2002) Digit ratio: a pointer to fertility, and health. Rutgers University Press, London

Martin B, Maudsley S, White C, Egan J (2009) Hormones in the naso-oropharynx: endocrine modulation of taste and smell. Trends Endocrin Metob 163–169

Melligard M, Vance Civille G, Carr T (2007) Sensory evaluation techniques. CRC press/Taylor & Francis Group, Boca Raton

Moss M et al (2003) Aromas of rosemary and lavender essential oils differentially affect cognition and mood in healthy adults. Int J Nerosci 113:15–38

National Institute of Health (2009) Smell disorders. From National Institute on Deafness and Other Communication Disorders: http://www.nidcd.nih.gov/health/smelltaste/smell.asp. Accessed 13 Mar 2010

Osmoz (n.d.). Fragrances. From Osmoz: http://www.osmoz.com/fragrances/Celebrity-Brands/Elizabeth-Taylor/White-Diamonds#. Accessed 12 Mar 2010

Perez-Cacho P, Rouseff R (2005) Fresh squeezed orange juice odor: a review. Food Sci Nutr 48:681–695

Pinel JP (2007) Basics of biopsychology. Pearson Education, Boston

Roberti J (2004) A review of behavioral and biological correlates of sensation seeking. J Res Personal 38:256–279

Roughgarden J (2004) Evolution's rainbow: diversity, gender, and sexuality in nature and people. University of California Press, Berkeley

Sobel N et al (2000) An impairment in sniffing contributes to the olfactory impairment in Pakinson's disease. Proc Natl Acad Sci doi:10.1073/pnas.071061598

Woltering R-J (2010) General manager, Sofitel Amsterdam The Grand (D. Derval, Interviewer)

Zuckerman M (1994) Behavioral expressions and biosocial bases of sensation seeking. Cambridge University Press

Chapter 4
The Right Sensory Mix

At the end of this chapter, you will know how to deliver the right sensory mix for each target customer. We dig into the intriguing world of touch and texture with *La Favorite,* and participate in the launch of new personal care services. You will design the perfect consumer experience, following the example of *Blacksocks.com.* And a framework will be given to effectively evaluate consumers' sensory profile and propose the winning sensory mix.

4.1 Introduction

In this chapter, we show how to design the right sensory mix for a product or service. In Sect. 4.2, we analyze the reasons that make consumers switch to a competitor with the hair case. The outcome leads us to explore the world of touch in Sect. 4.3. We learn the importance of textures in the consumer experience with *Blacksocks.com* and *La Favorite.* Winning firms are going the extra mile and provide consumers with useful tips, thus becoming their health, well-being, and lifestyle companion, as we demonstrate in Sect. 4.4. The key is to design the right sensory mix for each consumer group or to identify the best-suited target group for a given product, as we study in detail in Sect. 4.5 with the launch of new personal care services (Fig. 4.1).

4.2 What Makes Consumers Switch to Another Product? The Hair Case

Let us explore what makes a consumer switch to a competitor. With the hair case, we evaluate the respective role of price, consumer requirements, and recommendation in a consumers' decision to change supplier.

D. Derval, *The Right Sensory Mix*, DOI: 10.1007/978-3-642-12093-0_4,
© Springer-Verlag Berlin Heidelberg 2010

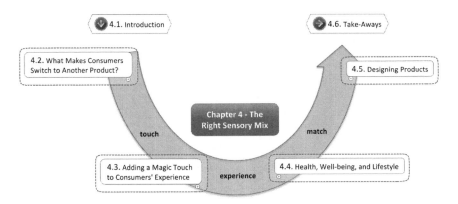

Fig. 4.1 Content of Chap. 4

4.2.1 The Price Fairy Tale

Our expertise was required in a sensitive product category: hair removal products and services. The question was posed in these terms: "Can you confirm that consumers switch to depilatory creams, electric epilators, or shavers, because of a competitive price?" For starters, the price of a waxing session is equivalent to the price of a cream or of an electric epilator. Knowing that the average hairy consumer might well need eight waxing sessions a year, this gives us a ratio of 8:1 between waxing in a beauty salon and using an electric epilator at home. This difference is huge. I started wondering why some women, and men, were still going to the beauty salon.

4.2.2 Unmet Requirements

Asking the question the other way around, and putting the price reason on hold, forced us to analyze the context more deeply and to understand the consumers' requirements.

The following criteria seemed to be the top consumers' concerns when considering a hair removal solution:

- Easy maintenance (fast cleaning, practical storage).
- Convenience (available on-demand, on-the-go).
- Effectiveness (how well the hair is removed, smoothness of the area).
- Lasting effects (number of days before the hair comes back, new hair texture and growth).

So, consumers in favor of depilatory cream are happy to be able to use it in the shower, consumers using a shaver or an epilatory device (like electric tweezers) appreciate its convenience as no appointment is needed, and consumers waxing do not want hair to grow back thicker.

Many consumers switched from solution to solution, testing everything from tweezers to laser, until they found the ideal fit, and others gave up experiments and selected the least uncomfortable option.

4.2.3 Birds of a Feather Flock Together

What made consumers try out a new product or service was the most powerful advertising: family and friends' recommendations.

Did you notice that birds of a feather flock together? So if you manage to deplume one bird, you might soon be able to pluck the whole flock. The key is to identify the orange-throated bird—our opinion leader and promoter. This promoter is so enthusiastic about the solution that he/she convinces many friends and relatives to at least try it. Then if they like it, they will naturally switch to it. To identify these precious clients, some companies use surveys asking consumers whether they would recommend the product, on a scale from 1 to 10 (10 being the maximum), and consider that the promoters are the ones answering 9 or 10 (Satmetrix 2010). We will see in the last section of this chapter that there are more reliable techniques for identifying promoters.

> Did You Know? Tomorrow, I Quit!
> If you observe poker players, you might see that, in addition to eating junk food and drinking alcohol (or Red Bull!), 8 out of 10 are smoking. Some might think that they are influenced by their friends proposing cigarettes. What neuroscience found out is that some people are just more likely:
>
> (1) to take the risk of smoking—because of a mutation in their dopamine receptor,
> (2) to become addicted to the cigarette—as they break nicotine down faster they need another puff to feel good, and then another.

So our poker players—typical risk takers—do not smoke because they are together but hang out together because they like the same things (Starr 2008).

4.2.4 The Painful Truth

But again, why are some consumers willing to pay eight times more for a hair removal solution? These consumers can of course afford the waxing sessions. What about the ones who can also afford the waxing sessions but prefer using a cheap epilator? Are they just being stingy? Also, if we remember what we learned from Chap. 3 on odorants, we can suspect that some women will never use depilatory cream because of the strong chemical smell. So maybe the purchasing decisions can once again be retroducted and predicted. We conducted over

50 in-depth interviews—we share the detailed results later in this chapter—and observed consumers being plucked (we did not go into the shower with them but almost). And the real motivations were revealed: it is all about touch.

4.3 Adding a Magic Touch to Consumers' Experience

Let us explore the secrets of touch, and see how firms can add a magic touch to consumers' experience when they grasp the power of textures, and shapes, following the example of *La Favorite* and *Blacksocks.com*. We will analyze the sensors involved in our hair case and find a sharp segmenting question.

4.3.1 The Secrets of Touch

The sense of touch refers to a variety of sensations, including change in temperature, pain, vibration, and movement. Our touch sensors cover our whole body with a special concentration on our tongue, hand palm, feet sole, genitals, and mammary glands (Marieb 2007).

In addition to free nerve endings (#1 in Fig. 4.2) and hair follicles (#7) sensitive to touch and pain, our skin hosts a multitude of sensors specialized in: light touch and pressure (#1), cold (#2) and heat (#3), strong pressure (#5) and vibration (#4 and #6).

Every square centimeter of our skin contains around 200 receptors for pain but only 15 receptors for pressure, 6 for cold, and 1 for heat.

Light touch, cold sensors, and hair follicles react fast, as their mission is to alert us to potential dangers. Heat, vibration, and strong pressure sensors sit deeper under the skin and take a bit more time to react to stimuli.

These millions of sensory receptors respond to external stimuli and send electric signals to our spinal cord and brain.

Fig. 4.2 Skin sensors (printed with DervalResearch permission)

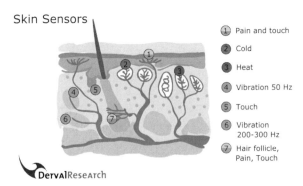

4.3.1.1 Light Touch and Pressure

Light touch, like contact with a woolen sweater, tickling on the skin, moving hair, or someone bumping into us in a queue, alerts us of the presence of potential danger. It tends therefore to be very irritating for people sensitive to touch—this sensitivity to light touch is called tactile defensiveness. On the other hand, a strong pressure like a firm hug, petting, or massaging tends to relax and calm animals and people.

Did You Know? Like a Squeezing Machine
A squeezing machine is used to calm anxious people suffering from tactile defensiveness. Being squeezed during 15 min has a relaxing effect of at least 60 min. Used on healthy people, the machine, composed of two mattresses, proved to have calming effects on 18 people out of the 40 tested (Grandin 1992).

4.3.1.2 Cold and Heat

We are programmed to perceive changes in external temperature in order to adapt our body response:

- 150,000 sensors reacting to cold or more precisely to heat loss are located right under the skin and concentrated in our fingertips, nose, and the bends of our elbows.
- 16,000 sensors reacting to heat and pain are located deeper under the skin and concentrated in our fingers, nose, chin, chest, forehead and lips (Human Physiology 3—The body's thermoregulatory system 2007).

Sensitivity to cold and heat is linked to hormones. While taking a contraceptive pill or having their menstruation, women tend to have an elevated body temperature, and are more sensitive to cold (Times Online 2008). Research measuring the threshold for heat and cold on 80 subjects, with the help of a thermal aesthesiometer, confirmed strong disparities between men and women, and between elder and younger individuals. Subjects were exposed to variations in heat or cold, and had to press a button to report their perception—the equivalent of the audiogramme discussed in Chap. 2 but for temperature. Women exposed to various temperatures on their finger, perceived them as cold starting at 27°C, whereas men perceived them as being cold only at 23°C (Seah and Griffin 2008, pp 535–543) (Table 4.1).

Table 4.1 Temperature thresholds in men and women

	Heat threshold (in °C)		Cold threshold (in °C)	
	Finger	Forearm	Finger	Forearm
Women 20–30	37.91	39.74	27.13	27.45
Men 20–30	41.92	43.70	23.28	26.56
Women 55–65	40.70	39.22	24.03	24.84
Men 55–65	44.19	43.52	21.87	25.74

Source: Seah and Griffin (2008, pp 535–543)

Note that our extremities dictate how hot or cold we feel. The temperature in our hands and feet might vary by 12°C.

Pain is a response to an excessive stimuli, excessive cold, heat, or pressure. When exposed to a cold pressor test, some people can tolerate the test for 300 s whereas others, very pain sensitive, will hardly be able to bear 50 s (Mogil 1999).

Did You Know? A Painful Haircolor

People with red hair are more sensitive to cold and pain. It seriously concerns the dental industry as red-haired people are twice as fearful of visiting the dentist than other people, who might already need some reassurance (Binkley et al. 2008). This hair color is in fact due to an excess production of yellow-red pigment–pheomelanin. It seems associated with a faulty regulation of cold and pain by the melanocortin receptor (Liem et al. 2005). Redheads also have a tendency to bruise more—and their sweat glands play an active role in thermal regulation (Liem et al. 2003).

4.3.1.3 Vibrotactile Perception

We saw in Chap. 2 that sound is a vibration. We perceive it via our inner-ear, but that is not all. Vibrotactile sensors covering our body are sensitive to low frequencies, especially around 50 and 250 Hz.

Textures are vibrations too. They are perceived by our tongue, as we saw in Chap. 1, but also by our hand palm, feet sole, and whole body. That is why in Chap. 1, super-tasters disliked the texture of fatty food.

You might have experienced these vibrations while traveling by car, working in an office, undergoing some drilling activities, or playing with a Playstation! Research shows that car motion sickness is mainly due to vibrations coming from the floor of the vehicle. The frequency that causes this ranges from under 1 Hz to over 300 Hz (Griffin 2007).

Did You Know? The White Finger of Vibration

Facing an increase in muscular, neurological and vascular disorders contracted at the workplace, the European Union released a directive to regulate the exposure to hand-arm and full-body vibration. A common injury is the *White Vibration Finger* due to poor blood circulation having as an effect destroying blood cells. So take it easy with your vibrating joystick! (Institute of Sound and Vibration Research 2006)

Here again, sensitivity to vibration depends on individuals. A good illustration is our reaction towards music. Some people are more likely to have goose-bumps than others, as was shown in an experiment. Thirty-eight subjects (29 women and 9 men) were exposed to 7 music tracks from Apocalyptica to Bossa Nova, and researchers measured the number of piloerections—yes, that is the scientific name of goose-bumps, another term for a 'skin orgasm'!—occurring during the song. The requiem "Tuba Mirum", composed by Mozart, generated the most piloerections. This 3 min tune starts with heavy tuba bass—those can go as low as 16 Hz—and halfway through the tune turns into a high-pitched singing voice. Differences between individuals were important: 17 did not show any piloerection, and among the 21 responsive ones, some had up to 15 piloerections per song! Both sudden increase in volume—*subito forte*—and unexpected modulation in frequency might provoke a piloerection (Grewe et al. 2007).

When performing a similar test on music students exclusively, the proportion of people subject to piloerection climbed up to 90%. Also the phenomenon is more often reported by women than by men, and by people not keen on taking physical risks (Huron 2006). So our orange-throated Red Bull drinkers are likely to be very resistant to 'skin orgasms'.

4.3.1.4 Touch Profiles

The perception of touch varies between individuals (Fig. 4.3).

Based on individuals' sensitivity to texture, touch, pain, vibrotactile signals, and temperature, we suggest to identify following profiles (Table 4.2):

- Super-vibrators: mainly women, sensitive to light touch, pain, variation in temperature and more likely to have piloerection.
- Medium-vibrators: prefer soft texture, sensitive to cold.
- Non-vibrators: mainly men, resistant to pain, cold, heat, and piloerections.

These touch profiles can be a great help in adapting clothing, packaging, consumer electronic products, and possibly painful operations, like our hair removal solution—as we will see later.

> Did You Know? Touch Your Clients!
> In an experiment conducted in a restaurant, the waiter would touch, or not, the arm of dining clients when bringing the bill. On average, touched clients left a tip of 17.5% whereas untouched clients gave a tip of 14.5%. So, touch your clients as much as you can! (Hornik 1992)

4.3.1.5 Textures

Texture is a vibration, and we perceive it through the movement of our fingers. The epidermal ridges forming the unique pattern of our fingerprint help us filter

Fig. 4.3 Touch profiles (printed with DervalResearch permission)

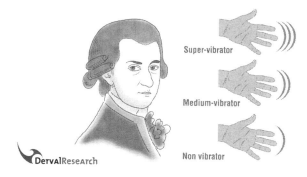

Super-vibrator

Medium-vibrator

Non vibrator

DervalResearch

Table 4.2 Detailed touch profiles

	Non-vibrators	Medium-vibrators	Super-vibrators
Textures	Unable to distinguish fine textures ($<200\ \mu m$)	Sensitive to textures, prefer soft clothing	Very sensitive to textures, picky on clothing. Prefer fine textures like cotton to synthetic or wool
Active touch	Can perform any manual activity (do it yourself, sailing)	Sensitive to activities involving strength	Very sensitive to sticky, sharp, grippy objects
Passive touch	Feel better strong pressure than light touch	Enjoy light touch	Irritated by light touch and relaxed by strong pressure
Pain	Resistant to pain, cold, and heat	Sensitive to cold	Very sensitive to pain, cold, and heat
Population	25%, mainly men	50%	25%, mainly women
Cold pressor test	300 s	150 s	50 s (6× more sensitive than non-vibrators)
Mozart requiem "Tuba Mirum" test	No piloerection	Less than 1 piloerection per minute	1 piloerection per minute and more

Based on measurements and observations performed by DervalResearch on 1,200 consumers between 2007 and 2010. *Additional sources*: Grewe et al. (2007) and Mogil (1999)

and amplify the vibration of the texture we feel—in a way similar to the way our inner-ear hair cells amplify sound, as seen in Chap. 2. These vibrations, around 250 Hz—the equivalent of the middle C at the piano—are processed by our vibration sensors, the Pacinian corpuscles, located deeper under the skin (#6 in Fig. 4.2). The corresponding signals are sent to our brain.

Texture can be characterized by following attributes (Chen et al. 2009):

- Warm/cold
- Slippery/sticky
- Smooth/rough
- Hard/soft
- Bumpy/flat
- Wet/dry

It is possible to measure the texture index—the acoustic vibration of the texture—with the help of a piezoelectric sensor. This device measures the acoustical vibration emissions of textures. In a cabbage variety benchmark, researchers were able to compare the texture of spring and winter cabbage by using a probe to penetrate a sample of their outer leaves. As the texture index of food increases after storage, the analysis enabled also to retrieve information on the cabbage shelf-life and storage (Taniwakia and Sakuraib 2008).

> Did You Know? High-pitched Fruits
> The texture index of apples and persimmons is much higher than the index of pears (Taniwaki et al. 2006). Particularly in the speech area, between 2,240 and 3,200 Hz. This explains why our super-amplifier in Chap. 2 often reported being annoyed by eating noise. Now we know why the sound of biting an apple is so distinctive.

Men and women with a shorter index finger have a greater sense of touch (Bai 2009).

Recent research among 100 college students showed the ones with a shorter index finger were better at identifying whether a pattern was with horizontal or vertical grooves (Peters et al. 2009). This indicates to me that very-testosterone oriented people are sensitive to texture and touch. This hypothesis confirmed by the fact, remember from Chap. 2, that Asperger sufferers, who had been exposed to prenatal testosterone, are very sensitive to clothing and light touch.

A study comparing the perceived softness of 20 distinct tissues shows how strong these disparities are. Ninety men and women were asked to evaluate how soft each tissue was and to tell for each evaluation how confident they were about their evaluation. The sample of answers published shows that one subject (S29) found that 14 tissues out of the 20 were 'not soft' whereas another (S45) evaluated only 3 tissues as 'not soft'.

Based on our touch profiles, subjects S1 and S45 are likely to be non-vibrators, as they have difficulty evaluating the softness of a tissue, with respectively 15 and 8 tissues not categorized, and only 2–3 tissues evaluated as 'not soft'. Subjects S3, S8, and S14 had more confident answers with 7–8 tissues perceived as 'not soft' and are likely to be medium-vibrators. And subject S29, who had very confident

Table 4.3 Tissue softness evaluation by mechanical stylus scanning (Rust et al. 1994)

Subjects	Not soft	Soft	Do not know
S3	8	6	6
S8	7	9	4
S14	8	6	6
S29	14	3	3
S45	3	2	15
S1	21	10	8

evaluations and 14 tissues considered as 'not soft', is very likely to be a super-vibrator (Table 4.3).

Did You Know? Biometric Touch Sensors
   Researchers are now able to simulate, with biometric sensors, the way our fingers respond to vibrations when they identify fine textures. Soon we could be able to touch clothing before ordering them over the Internet! (Scheibert et al. 2009)

4.3.2 Do Mosquitos Like You?

So if we think of our hair removal problem, consumers' behavior will be greatly influenced by their vibrator profile and their associated sensitivity to light touch or pressure, cold or heat, and pain. The other key criteria is their hair, of course!

The density and texture of their hair will have a direct impact on the perceived pain. Each hair follicle is connected to a nerve ending, which helps to perceive pain. Hair also alerts us of the landing of insects (useful in detecting mosquitos).

We can distinguish two types of hair, the vellus and the terminal hair:

- Vellus hairs are thin (<0.1 mm) short (<2 cm), and sometimes pigmented. Our whole body is covered with vellus hair except our hand palms, feet soles, parts of the genitalia.
- Terminal hairs are thick (up to 0.6 mm), long (>2 cm) and pigmented.

In fact, most of us were born with only vellus hair. Under the influence of hormones, in some individuals, vellus hairs turn into beautiful terminal hairs. The hair distribution pattern is also set by hormones. (Jankovic and Jankovic 1998)

Did You Know? A Furry Tale
   8% of women suffer from hirsutism and have terminal hair on their legs and arms. Testosterone and hyperinsulinism—an abnormal secretion of insulin causing hypoglyce-mia—seem to be at the origin of this usually male hair distribution pattern in women. Interestingly, 60–70% of diabetics are also very sensitive to pain. So our hirsute women are very likely to be super-vibrators (Greisen et al. 2001). Often linked with diabetes and obesity, hirsutism is also characterized by a deep voice and acne at puberty. A compen-sation is that hirsute women also have an increased sex-drive. (Dahlgren et al. 1998)

4.3.3 La Favorite, *Divans for Divas*

Talking about fur, let us study the success story of La Favorite.

I did not know whether I should share this case with you in this chapter on touch or in Chap. 5, on vision. Johan Bremer, who supported me in many of those 'crisis' situations, solved my dilemma by observing: "Shape is half-way between vision and touch".

Brigit Mettra, a former trader with a flair for luxury and design, identified a "niche" market: luxury furniture and accessories for Very Important Pets (Mettra 2010).

Instead of going the Paris-Hilton way with human-like mimics, she focused on pet-friendliness and home fit. Her master creation is the Sofa O'—an egg-shaped sofa for distinguished dogs. Shape, touch, and temperature were key when designing this product, that convinced pets, owners but also prescribers. Luxury Parisian Hotel *Le Meurice,* for instance, just announced that their clients will be able to comfortably house their furry friends in La Favorite's Sofa O'.

At the design stage, La Favorite thought of an egg as it is a universal shape— key for international expansion. Also, pets like to relax in a semi-closed space where potential predators cannot attack them from behind. Owners appreciate the 'home fit' of the white Sofa O', looking like a piece of art.

In terms of touch, the Sofa O' is made of porcelain. This hand-made material feels soft, but it is not boring because you can perceive some subtle asperities. Owners also appreciate that porcelain is of easy maintenance and very hygienic. Doggies benefit from the fact that this material keeps them warm in winter and refreshes them in summer. They are also comfortably supported on a warm and soft pillow made of fine and hypoallergenic cotton and acrylic. Owners can then, of course, match the pillow with their interior or thematic party (Fig. 4.4).

Target clients are wealthy families and luxury resorts. A typical persona would be an elegant woman in her forties, with a very good education, who enjoys traveling, contemporary art, and pets, of course! She loves the white color and considers Sofa O' as a piece of art—with a Dali-twist. She also very much enjoys the texture of the Sofa O'—a delight for super-vibrators, whether they are pets or owners.

4.3.4 Blacksocks.com, *When Socks Become a Luxury Service*

Sam Liechti, CEO of Blacksocks.com, built a sock empire based on a rather embarrassing situation (Liechti 2010). As a young executive, he was attending a business dinner in a Japanese restaurant. As the tradition requires, he had to take off his shoes, revealing the unthinkable: holes in his mismatching black (or dark gray?) socks.

Fig. 4.4 La Favorite (printed with permission)

This born entrepreneur then observed that:

1. Men do not want to spend time buying socks.
2. Assortments are often changing in retail so that it can be difficult to find your favorite socks again.
3. Nobody wants to be embarrassed because of worn out socks.

With Blacksocks.com, purchasing socks becomes as easy as having milk or newspapers delivered: every 4 months, you receive an envelope by mail containing three valuable pairs of socks—it is your Sockscription^{TM}.

Blacksocks has been a leader in this business for 10 years and has sold over 1 million socks. They plan to keep each client. Their secret to success consists in not giving clients any reason to switch to competitors. And it works. Many competitors failed in this sock business as they thought it was just about putting socks in envelopes. In fact, the Swiss company developed a whole sock experience with:

• Quality products—Blacksocks.com won several quality tests.
• Tips—the delivery form is more of a personalized letter with information on the product and tips on how to follow 'etiquette' (good manners for gentlemen). For instance 'etiquette' says that socks should be darker than pants.
• Service—the after-sales service is available for any question or suggestion. Each request is considered with the highest attention.

The socks are produced in Italy with an ideal mix of "chafe resistance, non-slippage, color-fastness, and odor absorption". Fifteen percent of purchases are gifts, with funny offerings like the "magic box", the solution to get rid of your partner's unwanted old socks. He/she receives an empty box to fill with all the socks falling apart, sends it back to Blacksocks.com and receives the same number of socks back, but they are new! On top of that, the old socks are recycled.

Many men order directly, and benefit from very targeted partnerships, like with Miles and More for instance. Thirty-three percent of the new clients were recommended and 25% of the clients become real promoters.

As the firm was expanding internationally—the U.S. represent their second market—they noticed differences in purchasing behavior:

• Germans prefer thicker Peruvian cotton socks.
• French prefer thinner Mercerised cotton socks, also called 'fil d'écosse'.

The favorite texture is more dependent on clothing habits than on weather or seasonality. Men preferring thicker socks are wearing sneakers while men preferring thinner socks are wearing business shoes. What about sensory perception? Let us ask a super or a medium-vibrator to compare both socks. The outcome is that the Peruvian cotton is smoother than the Mercerised one.

Interestingly, Germans have a long history of foot sensitivity—remember Einstein's socks in Chap. 2!—encouraging the development of major foot-friendly brands like Birkenstock sandals. Other benefits of thicker cotton socks, in addition to being soft, is that they protect and maintain the foot—limiting light touch—and absorb sweat very effectively. And we saw previously with our red haired example, people sensitive to touch also bruise more: quod erat demonstrandum (Q.E.D.)—which had to be demonstrated!

Once again, perception is key in proposing the right sensory mix. Blacksocks is busy changing mentalities: 'one size fits all' does not work for socks as they must fit perfectly, and feel right!

4.3.5 Touch Profiles: Business Applications

As the sense of touch influences our perception of temperature, contact, and pain, the business applications are many, from targeted outdoor or indoor activities, to suited clothing. Here are some ideas:

1 Vibrotactile texture rendering for e-commerce.
2 Healthcare services for super-vibrators (red-haired, hirsutes, diabetics) to better manage pain.
3 Soft clothing for super-vibrators and medium-vibrators.
4 Vibrotactile color rendering for blind people.
5 Temperature alerts for elder people.

In Sect. 4.5 we study in detail the sensory profile of different consumers and see how the perception of touch directly influences their purchasing decision.

4.4 Health, Well-being, and Lifestyle

In this section, we see how firms can develop products and services that address increasing individuals' concerns: health, well-being, and lifestyle. We study the mechanisms between perception and purchase, learn how to integrate Ayurveda, and to design the Right Vibes, and ultimately become the consumer's BFF—best friend forever.

4.4.1 Perception and Purchase

In this book, we decided to put the focus on consumers, but everything we discussed so far applies also to the business-to-business industry. In fact, even when you try to sell to consumers, you face a complex buying center composed of a purchasing consumer (our *champion*)—with or without the support of the bank!—a household supporting, objecting, or co-consuming, and promoters. In the example of Blacksocks.com, the spouse can be so 'supportive' that she will offer her husband a 'magic box'. If not, he might hear about the Sockscription^{TM} thanks to a colleague promoting the service. In that case, given the price, he will probably be able to go for it without having to refer to his bank.

As in business to business, you have only one *champion*: the consumer for whom your product is a 'must have', the one that will try to answer other people's objections and convince the financing organizations. It is key to identify the champion and make sure the sensory mix perfectly suits him—in our example nice, soft, comfortable, and thick cotton socks.

Of course the whole *household* might have its say: "Why do you always wear black socks?", or "You could just buy your socks at the supermarket!", "Are you sure you are sweating less with these socks?" The challenge for the brand is to take into account the household's sensory perception too and make sure that the product does not bother them in terms of color, smell, sound, texture, or taste, so much that they would be opposed to the purchase. Another threat can be that, due to a limited budget, the household hesitates between a home theater or a dishwasher, or because in terms of timing, a *Wii* fits better than a sofa, as we discovered in Chap. 2.

Promoters require special care. In our sock example, one new client out of three has been converted by a *promoter* and here it is not a declared intention of sending clients, as measured with the Net Promoter Score mentioned earlier, but real existing clients sending new real clients, for real.

According to the Ayurvedic approach, *promoters* should be very easy to bribe with food—as our main sense is the sense of digestion.

4.4.2 Ayurveda, The Sense of Digestion

If Ayurveda is considered in Western countries as an alternative medicine, in India—where it was born around 2500 BC—this is a serious medical school, with trained practitioners. In Ayurveda, the body is monitored by a different sense than those we have reviewed so far: the sense of digestion. The idea is that our body is a digestion process with an input and an output. Fair enough! The way a diagnosis is made proceeds similarly to the Hormonal Quotient[TM] (HQ) presented in Chap. 3. It is based on the observation of individuals as a whole, by considering following parameters: immune system, sensitivities, balance, body measurements, diet, digestive capacity, age, and fitness.

In very detailed illustrations, Ayurvedic medicine explains, for instance, how to diagnose diseases based on the appearance of the nails and of the tongue—in Western countries doctors often ask us to show our tongue but I am not sure of what they do with this information. Cracks on the tongue can suggest a derangement in the colon, and white spots on the nails are clear indicators of zinc or calcium deficiencies. More interestingly, nutrition advice is also provided, depending on patients profile and on the type of food. You will find some of the listed pieces of advice in Table 4.4. A negative effect of ice-cream is known to be congestion. So the mitigation plan proposed is to eat some clove or cardamon (Lad 1984). Vanilla-cardamon ice-cream, maybe the next Häagen-Dazs flavor?

Recommendations refer also to lifestyle, with the practice of Yoga or to the use of colors. So remember, blue is relaxing and orange is good for the sex-drive.

Table 4.4 Ayurvedic nutrition mitigation plans (Lad 1984)

	Negative effects	Mitigation
Ice-cream	Increases mucus, causes congestion	Clove or cardamon
Red meat	Heavy to digest	Cayenne or chili pepper
Green salad	Produces gas	Olive oil with lemon juice
Chocolate	Stimulant, depresses the system	Cumin

4.4.3 The Right Vibes

We were heading to a club with a group of friends (this part of the story is fictive—remember from Chap. 2, I am a bit autistic and do not have so many friends!), and when we arrived, one of them objected: "This place does not have good vibes". I decided to investigate these mysterious vibes. Also because I have heard it about people too, as in "This guy has bad vibes, I don't like him".

Maybe it is time for some retroduction. Sound is a vibration, expressed in frequencies. Touch is a vibration. Taste can be perceived as a texture—we saw the example of fatty food in Chap. 1—and texture is a vibration. We will see in Chap. 5 that vision is also traveling via frequencies. Some researchers recently highlighted that odor is a vibration too (Ai 2010).

> Did You Know? Listening to Rammstein's "Du Hast" is like receiving a massage. The main notes are indeed in the 50 and 250 Hz area, and therefore directly stimulate our vibration sensors throughout the whole body.

Based on these data, I would formulate the hypothesis that we are—just like amebas with their vibratile cilias—living entities that can perceive vibrations, or frequencies—let us call them vibes. Amazingly, in 1704, Newton, the first inventor who became famous thanks to an apple, retroducted that there was a link between colors and music. He suggested that propagation of light and sound were similar, and that they should be combined harmoniously (Newton 1704). He considered colors as corpuscles, more or less deflected depending on their size—red being the largest and violet the smallest. We will see in Chap. 5 that Newton was truly a visionary. In his Color Circle (Fig. 4.5), he ordered colors depending on their size and did a mapping between his seven primary colors and musical notes according to the Dorian musical scale. Each segment is proportional to the intensity of the related color. White is at the center. The C note, for instance, is at the border between violet and indigo. So when you play bass music in the B notes area (around 31 Hz), make sure you put a relaxing blue light on.

Not only do we absorb vibrations but we emit some too. In the same way that our inner-ear produces otoacoustic emissions when we hear a sound, as detailed in Chap. 2, our brain produces different brainwaves, depending on our level of activity. No, it is not a joke, you can really hear people think (or not!). During the thinking process, we are likely to produce Beta waves, between 12 and 30 Hz, as measured by electroencephalographies. When we are sleeping, the frequencies might be lower than 4 Hz (Niedermeyer and Lopes da Silva 2004) (Table 4.5).

Fig. 4.5 Newton's color circle (Newton 1704)

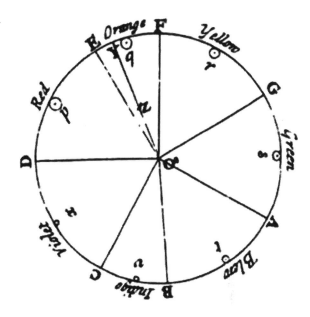

Table 4.5 Brainwaves

Type	Frequency (Hz)	Activity
Delta	Up to 4	Sleep
Theta	4–7 Hz	Relaxation
Alpha	8–12 Hz	Alert, Working
Beta	12–30 Hz	Thinking, Anxiety
Gamma	30–100 Hz+	Short term memory, Objects recognition, Sound, Touch

Adapted from Niedermeyer and Lopes da Silva (2004)

So individuals thinking too much or being anxious might indeed have 'bad vibes', above 30 Hz, so much that people do not want to be their BFF. Does this also apply to brands and products?

4.4.4 Becoming Consumers' BFF

The objective of each firm should be to become its target consumers' best friend forever (BFF). How to achieve this ambitious goal? The first step consists, without any doubt, in delivering the right sensory mix. A step further could be in making consumers feel good. Advising consumers on their lifestyle, well-being, and health, is a strong and binding added value.

We can think of Nestlé in New Zealand proposing differentiated nutrition advice sheets adapted to the sports you practice, similarly to Ayurveda, under the title "eating for your sport": rugby, swimming, triathlon, water polo, and more (Nestlé New Zealand 2010). Swimmers, for instance, are invited to eat a banana before the morning training whereas rugby men are advised to go for muesli at breakfast.

On http://www.betterimmunesystem.org, you can check your Hormonal Quotient^{TM} (HQ) and identify if you, or your children, are more at risk regarding food allergies. People very influenced by testosterone or estrogen, for instance, are reporting more allergies and food-related disorders.

As we saw in Chap. 2, organizations like London Metro and Dutch Railways deploy efforts to make their consumers feel safe and relaxed, using music and light, and we will continue investigating this in Chap. 5. Brands like Nintendo go even further and heal consumers! Wii Fit is widely prescribed by physicians for a faster recovery after an injury or in diseases like Parkinson's. And Wii Vitality Sensor positions itself as a health monitoring tool. The Nintendo DS, pre-installed with *Brain Age* becomes the most popular Alzheimer's prevention tool—in case it does not have any impact on the disease, at least it is fun to play.

In the pyramid of being the consumer's BFF, firms can basically go from giving useful advice to saving consumers' lives, the basics being to design products with the right sensory mix.

4.5 Designing Products: the Sensory Profiles

Designing products is all about the user experience. In this section, we will see how consumer sensory profiles can help us match or design the right products, with the example of an innovative hair removal solution. Also we will try to understand which features are core, and which ones are peripheral. We will review the design and testing process to make sure the end product is still on track.

4.5.1 It Is All About User Experience

Let us go back to our hair removal example. The fact that some consumers are not fully satisfied with the existing solutions offers room for innovation. Together with Emmanuelle Sangouard, hair care expert, who launched several prestigious brands for L'Oréal and Unilever in Benelux—including Elsève, Garnier, and Dove—we studied the response of 54 consumers to a new way of removing hair, in an experiment conducted in a beauty salon in Brussels. The participants accepted being observed and measured during the hair removal process, and they answered some questions so that we could identify their type of hair, hair removal habits, and frequency, preferences, and Hormonal Quotient^{TM} (HQ) (Table 4.6).

The new hair removal solution tested is based on a sticky fruit paste applied cold on the skin and removed in little firm massage movements, taking away the hair. The main benefits of this innovative solution, as perceived by the 54 consumers, are:

Table 4.6 New hair removal solution promoters per Hormonal Quotient™ (HQ)

	Promoter		Loyal	Regular	Occasional	Total Group	
Very-Testosterone	2	28.6%	2	1	0	5	9.3%
Testosterone	1	14.3%	14	0	0	15	27.8%
Balanced	4	57.1%	10	14	4	32	59.2%
Estrogen	0	0.0%	0	1	1	2	3.7%
Total	7	100.0%	26	16	5	54	100.0%

Research conducted by DervalResearch on 54 women in 2010

b1. The fruit paste is 100% natural.
b2. The hair is removed in a way that limits the in-growth.
b3. The hair grows back later.
b4. The hair grows back thinner.
b5. The hair removal is less painful (this is due to the simultaneous stimulation of cold and pressure sensors, diverting consumers from the pain!).

Very-testosterone-driven women are 9.3% of the clients and 28.6% of the promoters. It is an important group to consider, as half of the clients came upon recommendation. We see more balanced and estrogen-driven women among the occasional clients as they happen to shave in between visits, because it is more convenient or they have a special happening and want to be impeccable! Both very-testosterone and testosterone women are promoters or loyal clients—they do not want to consider any other way of removing their hair. Most clients are balanced women. They come more often as they want to be impeccable, like our persona Cindy.

Cindy is a body-hair maniac. She usually works in a bank, in finance, as a civil servant, a journalist, or a lawyer. She enjoys traveling and photography (Fig. 4.6). She used to wax every 4 weeks to be impeccable. Her eyebrows are a thin line. She does not own pets, but also sent her boyfriend to wax! She is bleaching a little

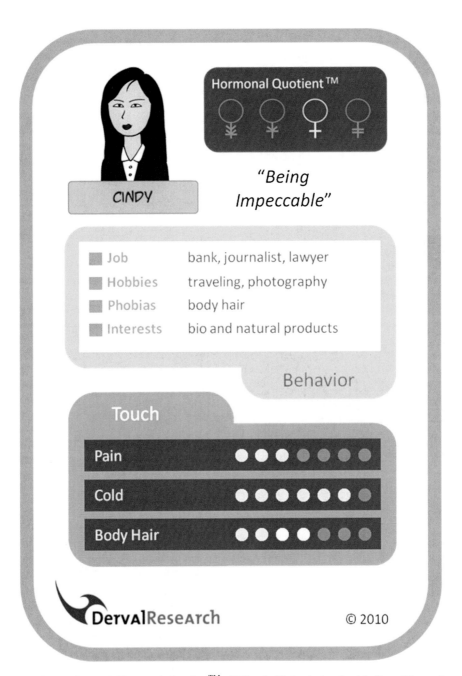

Fig. 4.6 Profile and Hormonal Quotient[TM] (HQ) of Cindy (printed with DervalResearch permission)

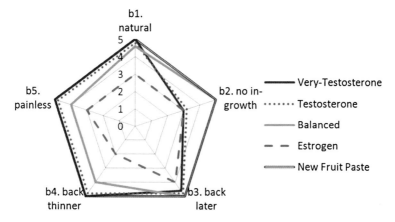

Fig. 4.7 New solution attributes and 'Must have' benefits per Hormonal Quotient™ (HQ)

moustache and thinks she is hairy like a monkey. When you have a closer look, you hardly see any hair–and she confirms that when there is a mosquito, it is for her!

She reports good health, and is quite resistant to pain. She has cold hands and feet. She tries to buy natural and bio products.

So for Cindy, having hair growing back later, benefit b3., is key. The fact that the removal is painless, b5., and that the fruit paste is natural, b1., is a definite plus. What won her over from the competition is that there is no hair in-growth, b2., especially around the bikini: a dream for our hair maniac (Fig. 4.7)

In comparison, for our testosterone-driven clients—often more furry—the most important is that hair grows back thinner, b4., and if the process can be painless, b5., it is very welcome.

Analyzing consumers' sensory profile helps us understand the success or failure of a product, and identify why some consumers are promoters, and others are regular clients, and also to match products with consumers.

4.5.2 Matching Products and Profiles

There are three ways of matching products and consumers:

a. We have a current product and want to target the consumers who would like it best (not recommended, but can happen!).
b. In order to win a consumer target group, we want to design the best suited product.
c. A bit of both! (which means that our product or service is flexible enough or that our target is unclear or flexible).

Now that we know the most important benefits for our group of consumers, we can compare other existing products on these criteria: waxing, epilator, shaver, and depilatory cream (Fig. 4.8).

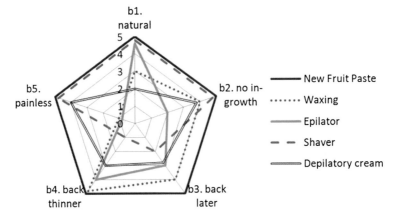

Fig. 4.8 Substitution products comparison

It appears indeed that the best current alternative for testosterone-driven women is shaving or waxing, good at respectively b5. and b4. For Cindy, putting b2. and b3. at the first place, waxing is the current best alternative.

Super-vibrators, often subject to hirsutism, will favor waxing or shaving. Medium-vibrators sensitive to in-grown hairs, will favor waxing or shaving. Other medium-vibrators and non-vibrators will use epilator or depilatory cream—if they are also non-inhalers!

By proposing a less painful, hypoallergenic, and anti-in-grown hair alternative, the new hair removal solution is likely to attract current waxing and shaver users.

By the way, this new hair removal massage is 20% more expensive than a traditional waxing session, and this has never been mentioned or highlighted by any of the clients. Consumers' perception is not only based on the hair removal itself, of course, but also on other features, core or peripheral, that firms could consider and integrate in their offering.

4.5.3 Core versus Peripheral Features

When analyzing a user sensory experience, we have to consider the whole experience, including the *core* features, the *peripheral* features, and any event that might happen to the consumer in between.

In our hair removal example, the *core* features are: the hair removal, and the massage, as it is expected, and to some extent the oil applied after the massage as it disinfects the skin, thus preventing the eruption of spots and other epidermal disgraces.

The *peripheral* features include the music, the light, and possible incense burning while the consumer is being treated. What determines if a feature is core or peripheral are the consumer expectations, based on solutions currently used. An ex-shaver will, for instance, consider music and light as a plus whereas a waxer-

Fig. 4.9 Core and peripheral services (DervalResearch 2010)

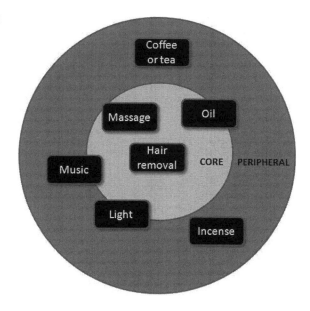

on-rehab is accustomed to a certain standard in beauty salons, including a welcome coffee or tea.

Similarly to the automotive industry, *peripheral* features are options that give firms the opportunity to test variations. Our beauty expert can adapt the oil to the Hormonal Quotient^{TM} (HQ) of the client: lavender for estrogen-driven profiles, and orange for testosterone-driven ones. And also, no incense for super-inhalers, as analyzed in Chap. 3. The successful *peripheral* features aspire to become *core*. Our beauty expert will then have to think of new options to delight the consumers, such as driving them back home or adding a cookie to the coffee (Fig. 4.9).

4.5.4 Designing and Testing

Designing is about the content, the container, and the process.

The Hormonal Quotient^{TM} (HQ) helped us group consumers in homogeneous segments, with similar sensory perceptions, and perceived benefits. And also similar job and hobbies, which can help reach and convert clients easily.

The comparison of a detailed sensory profile per Hormonal Quotient^{TM} (HQ) and solution helped us make the best match. A good point is that we only have to do this consumer profile analysis once. Then whatever new product we plan to release, we can refer to the sensory profiles to validate its relevance. A small panel of consumers, provided they have the same Hormonal Quotient^{TM} (HQ) will be enough to test the new solution.

Note that testing is a validation, not a discovery process—otherwise it is very expensive and risky! Knowing exactly what the target consumers perceive, and what they like/dislike in alternative products makes it much easier to design the right sensory mix.

In this chapter, we saw how to match products and profiles. In Chap. 5, we will see how to increase the innovation hit rate by using an innovation roadmap.

4.6 Take-Aways

Churn

- Price is not the real problem: It can make consumers try but not stay.
- Identifying and encouraging real promoters is key.
- Observing and questioning is more effective than chasing hidden needs.

Touch

- Texture is a vibration.
- Super-vibrators, medium-vibrators, and non-vibrators have a different perception of temperature, touch, and pain.
- A non-vibrator will be six times more resistant to pain than a super-vibrator.

Well-being

- Consumers perceive and emit vibrations.
- Selling to consumers involves a complex buying center composed of a champion, a household, banks, and promoters.
- Delivering the Right Sensory Mix is the least a firm can do, becoming consumers' best friend forever, relaxing them or improving their health and well-being is a plus.

Designing products

- We can use the Hormonal Quotient^{TM} (HQ) to identify promoters and loyal consumers.
- Sensory profiles help match products and consumers.
- The user experience includes the core features, the peripheral features, and all events the consumer will encounter during the consumption process.

References

Ai H (2010) Vibration-processing interneurons in the honeybee brain. Front Syst Neurosci 3(19):1–10
Bai N (2009) Fingerprints are tuned to amplify vibrations and send info to the brain. Available from Discover: http://blogs.discovermagazine.com/80beats/2009/01/30/fingerprints-are-tuned-to-amplify-vibrations-and-send-info-to-the-brain. Accessed 3 April 2010

Binkley C, Liem I, Gregg R, Neace W, Sessler D (2008) Increased dental anxiety, fear & care avoidance in Red Heads. In: International Association for Dental Research annual conference. IADR, Toronto, p 301

Chen X, Shao F, Barnes C, Childs T, Henson B (2009) Exploring relationships between touch perception and surface physical properties. Int J Design 3(2):67–77

Dahlgren E, Landin K, Krotkiewski M, Holm G, Janson P (1998) Effects of two antiandrogen treatments on hirsutism and insulin sensitivity in women with polycystic ovary syndrome. Hum Reprod 13:2706–2711

Grandin T (1992) Calming effects of deep touch pressure in patients with autistic disorder, college students, and animals. J Child Adolesc Phychopharmocol 2(1):63–72

Greisen J, Juhl C, Grof T, Vilstrup H, Jensen T, Schmitz O (2001) Acute pain induces insulin resistance in humans. Anesthesiology 95(3):578–584

Grewe O, Nagel F, Kopiez R, Altenmuller E (2007) Listening to music as a re-creative process: physiological, psychological, and psychoacoustical correlates of chills and strong emotions. Music Percept 24:297–314

Griffin M (2007) Discomfort from feeling vehicle vibration. Vehicle Syst Dyn 45(7–8):679–698

Hornik J (1992) Tactile stimulation and consumer response. J Consumer Res 19:449–458

Human physiology 3—The body's thermoregulatory system. Available from Healthy Heating: http://www.healthyheating.com/Thermal_Comfort_Working_Copy/HH_physiology_3_skin_sensors.htm. Accessed 3 April 2010

Huron D (2006) Sweet anticipation. MIT Press, London

Institute of Sound and Vibration Research (2006) Risks of occupational vibration exposures. University of Southampton, Southampton

Jankovic S, Jankovic S (1998) The control of hair growth. Dermatol Online J 4(2):2

Lad V (1984) Ayurveda: the science of self healing. Lotus Press, Twin Lakes

Liechti S (2010) CEO of Blacksocks.com. (D. Derval, Interviewer)

Liem E, Hollensead S, Joiner T, Sessler D (2003) Women with red hair report a slightly increased rate of bruising but have normal coagulation tests. American Society of Anesthesiologists. IARS, San Francisco

Liem E, Joiner T, Tseuda K, Sessler D (2005) Increased sensitivity to thermal pain and reduced subcutaneous lidocaine efficacy in Redheads. Anesthesiology 102(3):509–514

Marieb EN (2007) Human anatomy and physiology, 7th edn. Pearson Education, San Francisco

Mettra B (2010) CEO La Favorite. (D. Derval, Interviewer)

Mogil J (1999) The genetic mediation of individual differences in sensitivity to pain and its inhibition. Proc Natl Acad Sci USA 96:7744–7751

Nestlé New Zealand (2010) Eating for your sports. Available from Nestlé New Zealand: http://www.nestle.co.nz/Nutrition/SportsNutrition/NutritionAdviceSheets/Default.htm. Accessed 6 April 2010

Newton I (1704) Opticks. Smith & Walford, London

Niedermeyer E, Lopes da Silva F (2004) Electroencephalography: basic principles, clinical applications and related fields. Lippincot Williams & Wilkins

Peters R, Hackeman E, Goldreich D (2009) Diminutive digits discern delicate details: fingertip size and the sex difference in tactile spatial acuity. J Neurosci 29:(50)15756–15761

Rust J, Keadle T, Allen D, Shalev I, Barker R (1994) Tissue softness evaluation by mechanical stylus scanning. Textile Res J 64(3):163–168

Satmetrix (2010) How to calculate your score. Available from Net promoter: http://www.netpromoter.com/np/calculate.jsp. Accessed 23 March 2010

Scheibert J, Leurent S, Prevost A, Debregeas G (2009) The role of fingerprints in the coding of tactile information probed with a biomimetic sensor. Science 323

Seah S, Griffin M (2008) Normal values for thermotactile and vibrotactile thresholds in males and females. Int Arch Occup Environ Health 81:535–543

Starr B (2008) Ask a Geneticist. Available from Stanford School of Medicine The Tech: http://www.thetech.org/genetics/ask.php?id=134. Accessed 22 March 2010

Taniwaki M, Hanada T, Sakurai N (2006) Device for acoustic measurement of food texture using a piezoelectric sensor, vol 50. Faculty of Integrated Arts and Sciences, Hiroshima University, pp 739–8521

Taniwakia M, Sakuraib N (2008) Texture measurement of cabbages using an acoustical vibration method. Postharv Biol Technol 176–181

Times Online (2008) Why do women always feel colder than men? Available from TimesOnline: http://www.timesonline.co.uk/tol/life_and_style/health/article5106854.ece. Accessed 3 April 2010

Chapter 5
Increasing the Innovation Hit Rate

This chapter shows how business benefits from decisions based on scientific observations and gives guidelines on how to successfully implement this research method within the company and increase the innovation hit rate. Practical recommendations and business advice are shared by champion companies like *Björn Borg*. You will be fascinated by the secrets of sight revealed by *Carl Zeiss Vision* (Fig. 5.1).

5.1 Introduction

In Chap. 5, we share an approach to develop successful products and services. In Sect. 5.2, we see how to make sure these innovations are not only successful but sustainable by analyzing where the market is going, with the real estate case. The latest developments observed in the housing industry makes us dig into the world of vision in Sect. 5.3. We measure the impact of colors with *Björn Borg,* and share some serious eye-opening breakthroughs with *Carl Zeiss Vision.* We then have a look in Sect. 5.4 at the promising future of neurosciences. And we see in Sect. 5.5 how to plan success by including trends and technologies in product development roadmaps and organizing teams effectively.

5.2 Where is the Market Going? The Real Estate Case

Launching a product that is successful is good. Launching a product that is sustainably successful is better. Let us see with the real estate case why understanding where the market is going is key in increasing the innovation hit rate.

D. Derval, *The Right Sensory Mix*, DOI: 10.1007/978-3-642-12093-0_5,
© Springer-Verlag Berlin Heidelberg 2010

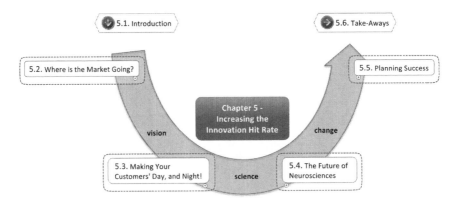

Fig. 5.1 Content of Chap. 5

5.2.1 Who is the Expert?

Our next mission brought us to the tough world of real estate. And the context was clearly presented: "We do not sell yogurt, we sell houses!" Luckily, we study people and not products—so our research approach seemed also appropriate in the case of houses and apartments sold off-plan. Target customers were defined as 'couple with a medium-to-high disposable income', and advertising placed in general newspapers was generating a lot of interest but very little sales. As the client was both building and selling the houses, the teams were concerned by two aspects: "How to better target customers?" and "Where is the market going?"

After a constructive meeting with marketing and product development teams, we decided to interview the experts: the teams in contact with customers—call center agents, and local sales representatives.

5.2.2 Moment and Perception

Call center agents were very happy to collaborate and share their expertise. They identified different purchasing moment, like senior citizens tired of taking care of their garden and wanting to move into an apartment. Another right moment was when young couples buy together, and get married to secure the investment—not very romantic, but powerful. Understanding customers' motivations was a good start but did not explain why, in the end, some customers bought the house and some did not. We suspected that the explanatory variable would be related to the fact that the house or apartment is built based on plans—within one or two years— and cannot be visited before purchase. We decided to investigate this further by interviewing the local sales teams.

5.2.3 Customers Could be Anybody

At the beginning of our one-to-one interview, the sales representative confirmed what we already heard from the marketing, product development, and call center teams: "Really, customers could be anybody."

We decided not to buy this answer, remembering that if we stop searching, we are certain not to find: "Sure, but if you would describe 80% of your customers—the ones who buy in the end—what type of people are they?"

Our open but tenacious questioning paid off: "Well, most of the time, people who buy are ICT engineers who studied in the area, aircraft pilots, or ···", and the sales representative listed seven embryos of personas. Top management was dubious—this was a bit too 'simple', plus "who would trust sales people?"—and required quantitative research to confirm the findings.

Marketing teams were busy writing a brief for a quantitative survey to be conducted on thousands of innocents when we said "Wait, there's no need for a survey, we can just make a query in the CRM database". For each sale, local teams complete a file in the Customer Relationship Management database. Most of the structured fields in the database were too generic—like the job title pick-list, limited to 'manager' or 'retired', "but easy to compute", as confirmed the IT team.

By chance, a left over field was secretly used by the sales team to enter fuzzy text, including the exact job title of the customers. With the help of text-mining tools, we grouped customers by different criteria like their job title, the area where they lived, the area where they bought the house or apartment, and were able to put figures in front of the seven now confirmed personas. For a given real estate program, one customer out of two was indeed an ICT engineer who studied in the area. For another program one customer out of three was an aircraft pilot. On the other hand, personas like Chris—our web designer of Chap. 1—were totally absent from the existing customer base. Understanding why, would help better target customers but also build relevant constructions in the future.

5.2.4 Market Prospective

ICT engineers for instance, always anticipate the next steps, and foresee limited mobility with age: driving or climbing stairs becomes more difficult and tiring. That is why they decide at some point to leave their house and move into an apartment in the city. Suddenly, the teams realized why a program that seemed totally adapted to this target group failed: an elevator was missing in the building! In the same way, scanning market trends is much easier to do when we have a specific customer in mind. For instance, our ICT engineer might be more receptive to solar energy than a history teacher, and more willing to pay a premium for such equipment. Thinking further of the differences between customers and non-customers, we found out why some people were more likely than others to buy a house just based on the construction plans. We were literally able to read the answer in their eyes.

5.3 Making Your Customers' Day, and Night!

In this section, we discover the secrets of sight. Perception of contrast and shapes is illuminated by *Carl Zeiss Vision*'s latest breakthroughs. We learn why consumers buy or wear funky underwear, with *Björn Borg*. And come back to our real estate case with surprising answers.

5.3.1 The Secrets of Vision

Light is a vibration of photons traveling at a high speed, around 300,000 km/s (Marieb 2007). Colors composing the light are absorbed or refracted in a different way by each object. This explains why a LEGO® brick will be red and another one will be blue.

Vision keeps half of our cerebral cortex busy and 70% of our sensors are located in our eyes, in the form of rods or cones (Marieb 2007) (Fig. 5.2).

- 120 million *rods* located on the periphery of the fovea help us see in the dark, distinguish shape, detect movements, and have a peripheral vision.
- 6 million *cones* located mainly in the fovea help us see at daylight, distinguish colors, details, and small objects.

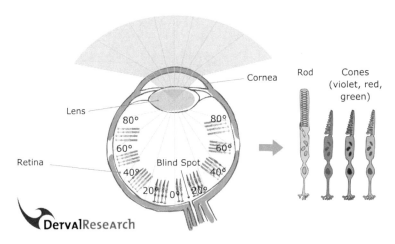

Fig. 5.2 Rods and cones distribution (printed with DervalResearch permission)

Depending on the level of light, we use our photopic, mesopic, or scotopic vision.

- Photopic vision is managed by the cones under day or sufficient artificial light, and allows a sharp image and color perception.
- Mesopic vision involves both cones and rods and is experienced at dawn or during full moonlight.
- Scotopic vision is managed by the rods and starts at low light levels when cones become ineffective. Rods are 100 times more sensitive to light than cones and get activated at dim light. Images are perceived in shades of grey and the acuity is reduced: a same object detected when 60 m away at daylight needs to be at 6 m under scotopic vision. As rods are a bit slower than cones we need at least 30 min to adapt in the dark (US 1/212th Aviation Regiment Flight Training Guide, Night Study Guide 2003).

> Did You Know? Blinking on Mr. Bean
>
> Research conducted on 9 Japanese men and 9 Japanese women in their twenties, showed that consumers tend to blink when there's no human presence on the screen to limit the loss of information in the action (Nakano et al. 2009). The subjects were exposed to visual torture: they had to watch a scene of the movie "Mr. Bean". Even if they all watched the video on their own and couldn't be influenced by each other, most of the subjects blinked at the same time: 64% of the blinking peaks happened when there was no human presence on screen, 6% at the end of a wide-angle shot, and 6% when the frame looked similar to a previous scene. The research also showed that some individuals blink 10 times more than others. Two subjects for instance presented an excessive average blinking of 64.5 and 43.9 per minute whereas two other subjects presented a low blinking with an average of 6.1 and 7.5 blinks per minute. The average blinking at rest is 22 blinks per minute. So asking a celebrity to promote your product on the screen does make sense—or at least it increases the chances the consumer's eyes are open when the message is displayed. A good start.

5.3.1.1 Color Perception: Di, Tri, or Tetrachromat?

The human eye can see colors with a wavelength between 400 and 700 nanometers (nm). Color wavelengths are higher than ultraviolet and lower than microwave radiation (Fig. 5.3).

Three types of cones help us perceive colors—each specializing in a range of wavelengths—violet, green, and red cones.

- Violet cones, or S-cones, detect short-wave colors like violet and blue.
- Green cones, or M-cones, are sensitive to medium-wave colors like green.
- Red cones, or L-cones, are sensitive to long-wave colors like yellow, orange, and red.

Rods are sensitive to black and grey.

Fig. 5.3 Cones sensitivity by color wavelength. *Source*: Adapted from Pinel, Basics of Biopsychology, Fig. 4.23 "The Absorption Spectra of the Three Classes of Cones" p.125, © 2007 Pearson Allyn & Bacon. Reproduced by permission of Pearson Education, Inc.

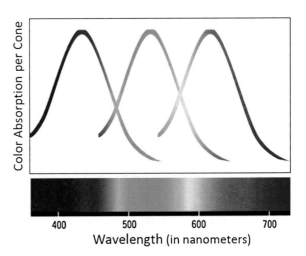

Contrary to popular belief, the primary colors, at least for human eyes, are violet, green, and red. Our eye works like a projector using these three primary colors to form more color nuances. For instance, blue uses 100% of violet cones and 20% of green cones. Yellow activates green and red cones equally. White is a combination of violet, green, and red cones.

But in how many colors do we see the world? Our color palette relies on the number of color beams used by our eyes. Dichromats, wrongly called color blind, are mainly men—in the United States they represent 8% of the men and 0.4% of the women— and they are missing a red or a green cone and have therefore a dog's life or at least a dog's vision: they see everything in blue, yellow, and grey nuances (Neitz et al. 2001).

When the red cone is missing they are protanopes. When the green cone is missing, they are deuteranopes. Red and green look both like brown, which does not help in activities like driving or decorating a Christmas tree.

Did You Know? Colors Lenses to Win

   Champions sometimes use color contact lenses to improve their vision and performance. Baseball players wear amber-tinted lenses to block blue light and increase the image resolution during actions. Golf players wear grey-green lenses to better distinguish nuances of green on the course (Hedge 2010).

On the other hand, recent research revealed that some individuals, 50% of the women, have a fourth cone, sensitive to wavelengths between green and red. Is it a second red cone? Or a yellow cone? This would explain some people's visceral reaction when confronted with this color. The opsin genes of 38 women were screened as they act as a predictor of the presence of this fourth cone and 23 women were identified as tetrachromat, and 15 were identified as trichromat. All subjects were exposed to a rainbow light and asked to distinguish the different chromatic bands they perceive. Women with four types of cones were on average able to differentiate 10 color nuances, women with three types of cones, were able

Table 5.1 Color nuances per chromacy	Chromacy	Color nuances
	Tetrachromats (four cones)	10
	Trichromats (three cones)	7
	Dichromats (two cones)	3

Source: Kimberly et al. (2001)

to identify seven nuances. Tetrachromats perceived on average more nuances in the wavelengths between 580 and 780 nm, which corresponds to the yellow, orange, and red colors (Kimberly et al. 2001).

Tetrachromats, like bees, see on average 10 different color nuances in the rainbow whereas the rest of the population, the trichromats, see only seven colors, and dichromats see three to four color nuances (Table 5.1).

You can check your color vision at www.derval-research.com

5.3.1.2 Contrast, Shapes, and Movement

The signals received by our senses, cones and rods, are computed, subtracted, and cross-checked, in order to create our visual perception, thanks to three pathways: the magnocellular or M-pathway (not to be confused with the medium wavelength cones!), the parvocellular or P-pathway, and the koniocellular or K-pathway (Stockman and Brainard 2009).

- The M-pathway transmits the signals from the L and M cones in an L + M form. This pathway specializes in luminance—remember green + red makes bright yellow—but also depth, contrast and movement as it conveys information from the rods (Gerardin 2005).
- The P-pathway transmits the signals from L and M cones in an L–M form. This pathway specializes in chromatic information, acuity, surface and shape recognition.
- The K-pathway integrates the input from the S cones in an S–(L + M) form. The K-pathway specializes in chromatic and luminance information.

Boys as well as girls exposed to prenatal testosterone show an increased interest in dynamic toys like a car and a ball. They are less attracted by toys like a doll, requiring nurturing. Tests conducted on vervet monkeys led to the same observations and confirmed that those preferences are innate and have nothing to do with social pressure or culture. Testosterone improves the M-cell pathway, that specializes in movement, and spatial processing (Alexander 2003). Now I know why I did not even screen the doll in Chap. 2 and went directly to the Playmobil Castle!

Did You Know? You Look Better with a Head Band!

You thought tennis champions like Björn Borg or Roger Federer were wearing a headband to absorb sweat or hold their long hair. Actually this headband is a visual reference that helps them aim better. Dyslexic individuals, who do not properly see shapes and words—the rods' information is altered because of a narrower M-pathway—noticed an improvement in their vision when wearing this fashion accessory (sharp-sighted.org 2009). You can experience this absence of visual reference illusion when you stare at someone's smoking cigarette in the dark street in front of a pub. You will have the impression that the little light spot is moving—and this has nothing to do with the couple of drinks you just had (Hussey 2003)!

5.3.1.3 Sensitivity to Luminance

The distribution of each type of cones in the retina, also called polymorphism, plays an important role in the color perception—especially with S-cones.

S-cones are the less numerous, around 7% of the cones, but seem very sensitive. M-cones should represent on average 25% of the cones and L-cones 68% (Calkins 2001). The average would consist in having 2.7 times more L than M cones. Based on gender, age, and ethnicity, very different distributions of cones have been observed.

A test conducted on 122 men and women in their 60s, 70s, and 80s, showed that the sensitivity of S-cones decreases with age, but faster in women (Eisner et al. 1987).

A comparison done on 27 African men, from Ethiopia, Ghana, Nigeria, Senegal, and Kenya, and 72 Caucasian men, from the USA, showed that African men could have from 42 to 85% of L-cones and Caucasian men from 37 to 95% of L-cones (McMahon et al. 2008). It would have been interesting to measure their Hormonal Quotient[TM] (HQ) to try to explain these huge disparities.

A group of 32 men and 33 women was shown a yellow light and had to mix a green and a red light together to produce the same yellow (Table 5.2). The differences in perception were huge, and women added on average more red (Pardo et al. 2007). Specialist *Carl Zeiss Vision* confirmed: tinted lenses are assembled manually and only by women as they are better at matching colors (Krug 2010).

A study conducted on two populations of bluefin killifish showed a link between the distribution of cones and the sensitivity to colors. The spring group have more S-cones and are more sensitive to shorter wavelength color, between 360 and 440 nm—UV, violet, and blue. The swamp group have more L-cones and are more sensitive to longer wavelength colors, between 560 and 600 nm—green and yellow. Researchers developed the hypothesis that species' cones distribution might evolve to adapt to the environment (Fuller et al. 2004).

Table 5.2 Color matching by gender

Red/green ratio	0.5	0.6	0.7	0.8
Women	14	16	8	4
Men	12	11	7	1

Source: Pardo et al. (2007)
Color matching test performed on 32 men and 33 women

Did You Know? No Blue for Diabetics

Some individuals suffer from a dystrophy of the S-cones and are tritan colorblind. Whereas a control group had 2,863 S-cones per mm^2, people with this deficiency had only 2,224 S-cones per mm^2. Also, in subjects with a normal vision, long-wave and medium-wave cones are separated by 20 to 30 nm, whereas in tritanopes the separation is of only 1 to 12 nm. The confusion in colors is directly related to the shift in the perceived color wave lengths. Rods are also suspected to interfere in color perception (Baraas et al. 2007). Many diabetics—almost half of them—experience a loss of S-cones over time that generates a tritan-like color deficiency. Diabetics suffering from this retinopathy perceive long and medium color waves 2.2 times less well than a control group and short-wave colors 40 times less well (Cho et al. 2000). So blue might not be the ideal color for diabetics!

You might have experienced this: you go outside, you are prepared to enjoy the sun and the fresh air when you start serial-sneezing. No, you are not victim of a tree allergy, this is a "photic sneeze reflex" due to a sensitivity to bright light! This particular sneezing—formerly called the "ACHOO" (Autosomal Cholinergic Helio-Ophthalmologic Outburst)—concerns 24% of the population. 10 photic sneezers and a control group were exposed to a bright light and Low Resolution Brain Electromagnetic Tomographies (sLORETA) were performed. The analyses revealed that in photic sneezers the bright visual stimuli activates also the somatosensory pathway—our highway to pain (Langer et al. 2010). So grandma's advice to look into the sun to start you sneezing might mislead 75% of the population.

5.3.1.4 Vision Profiles

Based on observations done on 1,200 consumers from over 25 countries, we propose to segment them into three groups: super-beamers, medium-beamers, and non-beamers.

Depending on their vision profile, individuals will have specific color and vision preferences (Fig. 5.4).

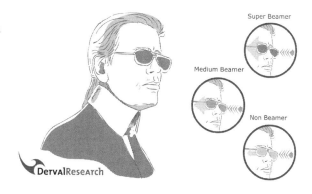

Fig. 5.4 Vision profiles (printed with DervalResearch permission)

Super-beamers are very sensitive to light, like our fashion star Karl Lagerfeld. He never removes his tinted glasses as they protect him against paparazzi flash and other bright lights. Super-beamers usually have four cones and are therefore sharp at matching colors.

Medium-beamers are less sensitive to light, and prefer medium wavelength colors.

As their cones are not overlapping too much, non-beamers do not mind bright colors like yellow (Table 5.3).

5.3.1.5 Auto-Focus and 3D Vision

The shape of the eyes and how they are embedded in the skull influence our ability to focus and to experience 3D vision.

F is the focal point of the eye, located at the back of the retina, where all lightwaves meet after passing the lens. The exact location of the focal point varies between individuals.

- Far-sighted people have a shorter eyeball and the F point is beyond the retina. Convex lenses help light focus on the retina.
- Near-sighted people, or myopes, focus light in front of the retina. Concave lenses help correct the focal point (Carl Zeiss Vision 2010).

Interestingly, the past 30 years, the proportion of near-sighted people in the USA increased from 25 to 41% (Vitale et al. 2009).

As we saw earlier, each color refracts differently on an object. This applies also for the eye. A violet light will arrive in front of the retina, a red light beyond the retina, and a green light somewhere in between. This phenomenon is called *chromatic aberration* (Fig. 5.5).

A muscle helps the eye change focus: tensing for near vision and relaxing for far vision. You can try the test with the illusion designed by Prof. Akiyoshi Kitaoka (see Fig. 5.6). It alternates violet, a short wavelength color, with yellow, a long wavelength color. Switching from one color to another might make you feel a bit dizzy—luckily this book is waterproof.

Did You Know? #0044CC is the Color of Money

It took intensive research for Microsoft to identify the best color to use to display results in its visual search engine Bing: blue (Chan 2010). "We wanted to try red links or brown links and no color," shares Bing's User Experience Manager. He adds that in the end "the science of clicks and art came together for blue." So far, just the science of optics and colors refraction would have been enough to draw these conclusions, and probably much cheaper. The good news is that Microsoft went the additional extra mile to confirm that most people—or at least the ones tested by the Seattle firm—prefer short-wavelength colors but not too short. The color generating the best click-through rates is a cornflower blue with undertones of purples: #0044CC.

Table 5.3 Detailed vision profiles

	Non-beamers	Medium-beamers	Super-beamers
Luminance	Do not mind bright light	Prefer dim to bright light	Very sensitive to bright light. Photic sneezers
Favorite colors	Like bright colors like yellow, and also blue, and black	Prefer colors like blue, red, green, or pink	Prefer colors like violet or blue
Focal point	Mainly far-sighted	Mainly near-sighted	Mainly near-sighted
Chromacy	Mainly trichromats, some dichromats	Mainly trichromats	Mainly tetrachromats
Cones distribution	Little cones overlap	Medium cones overlap	Strong cones overlap
Clothing	Dependent on relatives' help	Can wear various colors and patterns together	Wears perfectly matched colors and little patterns
Car parking	Few attempts	Many attempts	Try only in wide places!
Population	25%, mainly men	50%	25%, mainly women

Source: Based on 1,200 measurements and observations performed by DervalResearch in over 25 countries from 2007 to 2010

Fig. 5.5 Chromatic aberration (printed with DervalResearch permission)

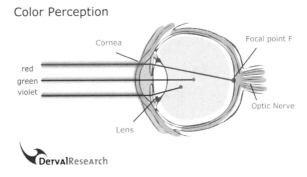

Fig. 5.6 Visual Illusion. Each border of adjacent turtles is vertical or horizontal, but appears to be tilted by the illusion of fringed edges and the turtles appear to wave. Visit Prof. Kitaoka's page on Ritsumeikan University of Kyoto's website for more illusions: http://www.ritsumei.ac.jp/ ~akitaoka/index-e.html. *Source*: "Baby turtles lightened by the moon" by Akiyoshi Kitaoka (printed with permission)

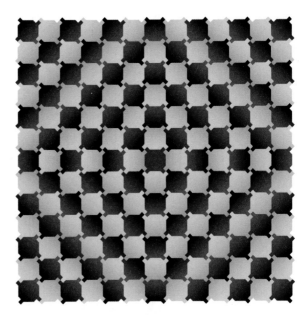

When we go to the cinema and wear 3D glasses, the effect is created by a different image received by the right and the left eye. Even without those glasses, we are able to perceive depth and perspective, because we receive an image from a different angle on each eye. The greater the 'binocular disparity'—consisting in having the eyes embedded in the skull in an asymmetric way—the greater the 3D vision.

5.3.1.6 Vision Modifiers

The size of the pupil, the thickness of the cornea, the blink rate, the shape of the eyes, and the visual context all have an influence on our vision. Due to a thicker structure in their eye, senior people receive three times less light than children (Hedge 2010). Pupils' dilation, for instance, occurs in cases of interest or danger. Pupils' constriction in cases of boredom (Marieb 2007). So if you suddenly notice the beautiful green iris of your colleague, he or she might just be bored to death looking at your 354 holiday pictures.

Nutrition and lifestyle also have an impact on vision. For instance smoking decreases night vision accuracy by 20%. A lack of vitamin A may also reduce night vision. So cheese, butter, apricots, and peas are good for your eyes (US 1/ 212th Aviation Regiment Flight Training Guide 2003).

5.3.2 Carl Zeiss Vision: *You Will Not Believe Your Eyes!*

If quitting cigarettes and eating cheese does not improve your night vision enough, you can now visit an optician who proposes *Carl Zeiss Vision* ophthalmic solutions and buy the revolutionary i.Scription glasses.

The leading vision glasses and lenses manufacturer, with a revenue of 880 million euro in 2009 and 12,000 employees worldwide, since the merger with Sola, started its activity 150 years ago with microscopes.

Inventor of the anti-reflective (AR) coating, Carl Zeiss Vision comes back today with another groundbreaking innovation. As we saw previously, different light wavelengths are focused by the eye with a different accuracy. These chromatic aberrations can cause an important shift in our color matching ability (Stockman and Brainard 2009). Carl Zeiss Vision uses a powerful diagnostic tool to optimize the focus for many points on the eye: the i.Profiler reflects small dots on the retina and recalculates the lens specifications to optimize the dots. The results are an improved color contrast and night vision. "The adjustment has to take other criteria into consideration than correcting vision: seeing stars so accurately that they just look like small dots is not very romantic anymore!", highlights Herbert Krug, Corporate R&D Director at Carl Zeiss Vision (Krug 2010).

The more irregularities you have with your eyes the more the correction is impressive. To give you an idea, here is the same night view with and without the i.Scription glasses (Figs. 5.7, 5.8).

5.3.3 Putting Things into Perspective?

Back to our real estate mystery. With the collaboration of Carl Zeiss Vision and one of their lead opticians, Frits Bijl, owner of the Kijkkamer, we decided to look into the eyes of a typical client buying off-plan houses: Bob, an ICT engineer.

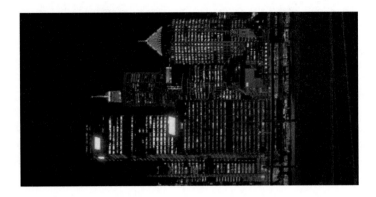

Fig. 5.8 Night view with i.Scription (printed with *Carl Zeiss Vision* permission)

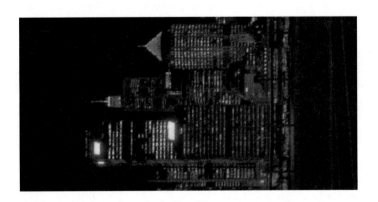

Fig. 5.7 Night view without i.Scription (printed with *Carl Zeiss Vision* permission)

Fig. 5.9 Bob the engineer's right eye—with high aberrations (i.Profiler analysis)

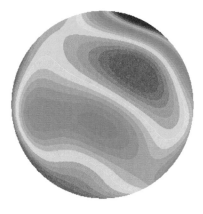

Fig. 5.10 Chris the designer's right eye—with low aberrations (i.Profiler analysis)

We also studied consumers, like our persona Chris, who only buy a house they can visit beforehand.

Bob is an ICT Systems engineer. He likes biking, running, and ice skating. He is wearing a complicated looking watch, with many indicators, but not too expensive. He likes the *Kjelvik* brand of outdoor clothing with dark jeans, a grey pullover, and trekking shoes. He drinks espresso, or chocolate milk, and listens to blues and country music. He used to play saxophone, guitar and accordion. Royal blue relaxes him and he does not like yellow or too lively colors. He enjoys holidays in sunny countries, and drives a Volkswagen Golf camper.

We were clearly in presence of a medium-beamer. The anamnesis confirmed that Bob is near-sighted: no wonder blue relaxes him.

Bob's right eye analyzed with the i.Profiler presents many aberrations as seen in Fig. 5.9. You can interpret the picture like a topographic map: the more you have mountains or valleys, the more you have imperfections on the eye called aberrations. To give you a comparison, in Fig. 5.10 you can see the right eye of Chris, almost perfect. In terms of night vision, it means that Bob sees our skyscrapers like in Fig. 5.7 and Chris like in Fig. 5.8. Under day light, Chris will also have a better perception of colors than Bob. By analyzing the eye of 49 subjects, their job, and Hormonal Quotient^{TM} (HQ), it seems that people working with colors (web designers, florists, fashion designers) are more estrogen-driven and have fewer aberrations in their eyes. Which after all, would make sense: who would trust a dichromat fashion stylist?

Anamnesis was made popular by Socrates. He believed that people already had all the knowledge inside and that teachers just had to help them remember. This particular way of questioning is always very powerful. After a couple of questions, Bob revealed the truth: he plays Trackmania every day and is ranked #93,000 worldwide among over 6 million players!

Trackmania is a racing game on the computer that takes place on fantasy tracks involving crazy stunts, jumps, loops, high climbs, and deep falls (Trackmania 2010). Players are the type of people who demonstrate sharp spatial representation skills. The type of people who would have no issue to imagine their house in 3D just based on a plan.

Bob presented more aberrations on the eye than Chris but also a greater binocular disparity. A spatial experiment conducted on 29 balanced men and 30 very testosterone-driven men, confirmed that prenatal exposure to testosterone had a direct impact on the ability to mentally rotate objects (Hines et al. 2003). The fact that Bob is very testosterone-driven would explain his strong spatial perception skills and aptitude to imagine his house in 3D just based on a plan (Fig. 5.11).

We studied the real estate and construction company's existing clients: the vast majority studied engineering and had indeed a very testosterone-driven Hormonal Quotient^{TM} (HQ)! To attract more consumers like Bob, the firm improved the connectivity in the houses—Bob can build his own local area network (LAN) effortless (and why not link the coffee machine to the garage door so that the cup is ready when he comes back home!)—and promoted the houses in specialized magazines for engineers. To attract more consumers like Chris, the firm designed new houses with more style, proposed more customization options—Chris can now design his own parquet floor, and create trendy bathroom and kitchen tiles—and invested in online virtual tours making it easier for Chris to imagine the house in 3D based on the plans. By increasing its innovation hit rate, the firm moved from number 2 to number 1 in its market!

5.3.4 Vision Profiles: Business Applications

Understanding perception of colors, luminance, shapes, and movement has huge potential in product development and commercialization.

1. Adapting colors and shapes to consumers depending on their Hormonal Quotient^{TM} (HQ).
2. Correcting consumers' chromatic vision with color lenses or glasses.

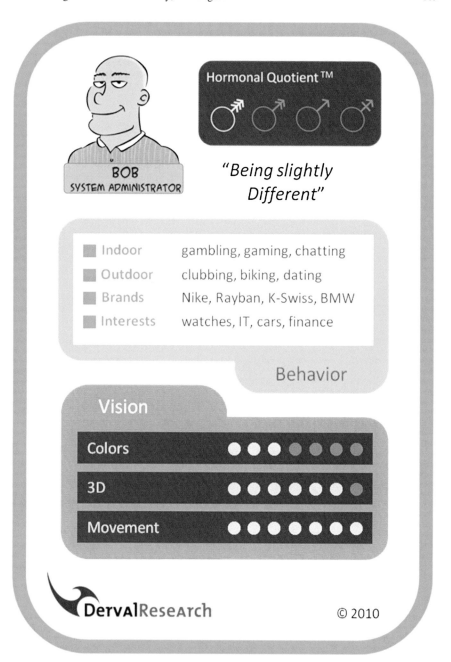

Fig. 5.11 Bob's profile and Hormonal Quotient[TM] (HQ) (printed with DervalResearch permission)

3. Improving lighting at the workplace and in public spaces for less luminance and enhanced shopping experience.
4. Accessibility to written material for dyslexics and visually deficient people.
5. Mastering light refraction to make objects invisible (or not!).

5.3.5 Björn Borg, *the Wimbledon of Funky Underwear*

Alan Greenspan, economist and former Chairman of the Federal Reserve in the USA, shared in the 1970s that the sales of men's underwear was a great indicator of financial health: in times of crisis, underwear was the last thing men would buy as nobody sees it (Colman 2009).

Today, not only men proudly display their underpants—mayors of major cities like Dallas even crusade for "pulling up pants"—but women offer them underwear (Goodwyn 2007).

Björn Borg, the head-banded Swede, was a bit the Roger Federer of the 1970s: a great champion, and a gentleman with style.

In 1984, he retired from tennis and created a clothing line with a focus on men's underwear and a vision: being "World champion in fashion underwear". The success of the underpants with trendy patterns and funky colors was immediate in Sweden, market leader, and is now converting the Netherlands, Belgium, and Denmark. Spain, Italy, Greece, and the UK are the next target countries (Brennicke 2010).

The brand licenses footwear, and glasses, but the focus is underwear with 70% of the sales for Him and 30% for Her. Fitting, texture, patterns, and vibrant colors are key. The 'Swedish Export' campaign makes consumers enthusiastic and they receive thousands of pictures of "ordinary people transformed by the power of underwear", even in extreme conditions like in the snow (see Fig. 5.12).

Current clients are Björn Borg and tennis fans, girls and boys at high school, but also young professionals, who practice jogging and running. The underpants are therefore mostly in cotton. "Underpants are also a seduction tool", confirms Rocky af Ekenstam Brennicke, Marketing Director at Björn Borg. More than 50% of the sales are for gifts.

A vendor confirmed that when buying men's underpants, men and women buy quite different models.

- *Men like low waist underpants.* Favorite colors are blue, yellow, orange, and pink. They enjoy funny pattern (like the trophy pattern, at the bottom of Fig. 5.12), and visible brand or Björn Borg face. They prefer a wider band, ideally white so that it sticks out from the pants.
- *Women buy men's underpants with a thinner band.* Favorite colors are purple, pink, and sky blue. Patterns with letters are popular.

We wondered why women like offering purple underpants to their partner, and followed them to the train station.

Fig. 5.12 Björn Borg "Swedish Export" campaign (printed with permission)

Table 5.4 Favorite color wavelengths per Hormonal Quotient™ (HQ)

		S-waves	%	M + L-waves	Total group	%
	Very-testosterone	5	20.0	1	6	13.0
	Testosterone	10	40.0	10	20	43.5
	Balanced	7	28.0	9	16	34.8
	Estrogen	3	12.0	1	4	8.7
Total		25	100.0	21	46	100.0

Source: Research conducted by DervalResearch, with the participation of NS (Dutch Railways) and Prorail, on 46 women traveling by train in the Netherlands in December 2009

5.3.6 Hormonal Quotient™ (HQ) and Favorite Color

Together with NS (Dutch Railways), Prorail, Davita, Ledhuren, and the Leiden train station (the Netherlands), we had the opportunity to analyze during 14 days the vision and waiting behavior of 1,004 travelers—590 men and 414 women—under different light conditions.

This research confirmed many biological and optical facts presented earlier and enabled us to make a link between hormones and color preferences.

Travelers preferred to wait for the train on a platform with a green, a red, or a violet light—rather than with a yellow or a white light. The respondents qualified green, red, and violet, as being warm colors. So maybe the real 'warm colors' are the ones heating up our S, M, or L-cones the most. They were also more relaxed with a blue light or no light at all. They preferred a red light with a high luminance or a blue light with a low luminance—which is consistent with the fact that short-wave colors are more visible at dim light. All the other lights, and especially red, look grey at night.

We measured the Hormonal Quotient™ (HQ) of 46 of the observed women and collected their favorite color (Table 5.4).

Very-testosterone and estrogen-driven women are more sensitive to long-wave colors like yellow and red, and to medium-wave colors, like green and black. 83%

of the very-testosterone and 75% of the estrogen-driven women prefer short-wave colors, and especially violet.

So our mysterious super-beamer purple underwear offerer is likely to be a very-testosterone or estrogen-driven woman. Interestingly, in a sample of 26 men, only two loved violet. So ladies, stop buying purple stuff for your partners, they just do not like the color so much!

5.4   The Future of Neurosciences

Understanding the human brain, the nervous system, and sensory perception offers incredible perspectives. An appeal for quantitative analysis among researchers puts the focus on brain and DNA slicing. We hope that research in neurosciences will quickly shift from "where" to "why" type of questions as there are so many observed phenomena to explain.

5.4.1   Science Versus Statistics

Pointing at a table full of percentages, my mathematics teacher told us once: "this has nothing to do with mathematics, this is statistics". He explained the major difference. Mathematics is about finding a model, based on observations, that was so robust and predictive that it was an exact science. For instance $2 + 2 = 4$, no matter if it rains or not. Statistics is about trying to support a more or less well interpreted observation with as many cases as possible, without trying to identify a model or isolate the context. So if you randomly draw 100 consumers from a supermarket that contains 1,000 consumers and 55 consumers like blue and 45 like red, two things happen: (1) you still do not know which color your product should be! And, (2) you have no clue, if you draw 10 other consumers, which color they will like. Of course, as their favorite color depends on their age, gender, ethnicity, country, shape of the eye, and aberrations—in other words it depends on their Hormonal Quotient™ (HQ), as we just saw. The main issue in statistics is the context and the representativity of the sample—remember the tasting panel full of non-tasters in Chap. 1. The attractive side of not identifying a clear model is that you can charge your client for a giant "quantitative research project" involving random drawings of thousands of consumers and asking them their favorite color. Statistics are used to quantify phenomenon that are not understood.

5.4.2   Brain Specialization and Development

There are over 100,000 million galaxies in the universe, about 100,000 million stars in a galaxy, and 100,000 million neural cells in our brain (Kraus 2005).

Each neural cell communicates information with up to 10,000 connected cells, and muscles, via electric impulse of 1 microsecond (ms) called *action potentials* (NeuroProbes 2010).

Most brain studies are busy with localizing activities thanks to functional magnetic resonance imaging (fMRI). It is about measuring changes in the blood flow in various parts of the brain. The idea behind this is that we send blood towards the areas that we need to perform our tasks. Researchers find out that most of the beasts, like birds, frogs, and mammals, manage their business in a very optimized way: their left brain hemisphere focuses on routine activities like eating while their right brain hemisphere is ready to face emergency situations like an attack (Vallortigara and Rogers 2005).

Did You Know? Brain Enlargement
   Species like squirrels, always remember the exact location they hid their nuts (Liang et al. 1994). A magnetic resonance imaging (MRI) study comparing the brains of 10 London taxi drivers with 50 non-taxi drivers, confirmed that the right hippocampus of the navigation professionals was bigger (Maguire et al. 2000). Soon, your spouse, who is always losing the keys, will be able to get a hippocampus enlargement !

Research conducted on 26 girls demonstrated that parts of the brain can indeed be reshaped. On the MRI, it appeared that the 11 girls playing Tetris 1.5 h per week during 3 months got a thicker cerebral cortex, on the parietal and temporal lobe, than the 15 control girls prevented from playing Tetris (Haier et al. 2009).

Another research project shows that the size of the neocortex is proportional to the number of connections apes have in their clique (Kudo and Dunbar 2001). Terrestrial individuals have a bigger network than arboreal individuals.

Before networking extensively, you want to check if your neocortex is able to manage your 500+ Facebook connections.

More attention is given to connections in general and to analogical thinking—maybe we are not the only ones retroducting? A recent paper suggests that when we look like we are doing nothing, our brain is busy making associations between data and objects we memorized in order to generate predictions (Bar 2007). Further research in that field could facilitate communication between retroducters and sequential thinkers.

5.4.3 The Brain Mapping Frenzy: From 'Where' to 'Why'

With the current brain mapping frenzy, be prepared to receive, instead of the traditional reports saying "55% of the consumers like blue, and 45% like red", "17% of the consumers had this area of the brain blinking when we showed the product, and 56% had this other area blinking"—which in the end does not help much more with understanding and predicting consumers' behavior, but is more expensive, given the cost of an MRI.

When the model is clear, you do not need to quantify anything: the same consumers, in the same context, systematically behave in the same way. It is similar to the laws of physics. I have a given weight on earth. I have another weight on the moon (much more advantageous by the way!). Understanding the 'why' is more useful, and often less expensive, than describing the 'how much', and the 'where'.

5.4.4 Disease Prevention, Vocation Finder, Dating, and More

Neurosciences and neuroendocrinology can help us improve our health and well-being. Some researchers are busy with the "why" and try for instance to solve observed phenomenon, like the "epileptic and the shoe smell". Among the 20 doubtful rituals people perform in Nepal to stop an epileptic seizure—I spare you the pet-unfriendly things related to sacrifices—smelling a shoe is very popular (Jaseja 2008). Epilepsy concerns millions of individuals—3 million just in the USA (Epilepsy Foundation 2010). A seizure is like an electrical shock occurring in the brain. The symptoms depend on the part of the brain affected and are often accompanied by convulsions. Seizures can be initiated by food ingestion, hormone fluctuations, and photosensitivity. It is not clear if sniffing a shoe can distract the faulty brain cells but electroencephalograms (EEG) confirmed that it really helps to stop the seizure.

As we saw in the different chapters of this book, sensory perception and hormones are major explanatory variables in consumers' behavior and preferences. Current knowledge in that field is also used as a decision support system to find the right nutrition plan, job, hobbies, or mate. We will even see in Sect. 5.5 that, depending on their Hormonal Quotient^{TM} (HQ), leaders will have a different approach to innovation.

5.5 Planning Success: the Innovation Roadmap

Once we understand consumers' preferences and are able to predict their behavior in a novel context, it is much easier to innovate. Only two things can go wrong at this stage: you miss major trends in the market and/or your senior management team does not understand your innovation. Here, with the example of the high-speed train, are some powerful tools and tips to plan your success.

5.5.1 Crystal Ball Versus Crystal Clear

We had an interesting prospective mission: "Where is the transport industry going?" Foreseeing changes that would arise in this market within, let us say the coming 15 years, might sound like a 'crystal-ball' exercise. Especially when you have in mind these yearly reports written by well-established institutes and that included statements like "by year Y everybody will use mobile phones for video-conferencing while walking" or "by year Y all firms will have implemented a Strategic Risks Management software". And you are already in year $Y + 20$ and none of those happened!

On the other hand, nobody told us that more and more public and corporate toilets would be equipped with cool Dyson hand dryers—you know the ones that look like a toaster for hands with wind blowing from all sides so that you do not have to rotate your hands like a fool anymore in order to dry them. As we were able to foresee the launch of the Wii Fit with our positioning map in Chap. 2, accurately guess Gary's smell preference in Chap. 3, and know with certitude in Chap. 4 that when there is a mosquito around it is often for Cindy, without asking her or interviewing the mosquito, why not accurately depicting where a market is going? Our hypothesis was that for each hazard occurring there must have been someone, somewhere, who knew.

5.5.2 The Expert and the Fool

What is the difference between an expert and a fool? Both predict events. People tend to believe the warnings coming from experts and ignore those coming from fools. Why? Because experts' forecasts are often more 'believable'. Typically, the expert would firmly say: "The increasing awareness of consumers about environmental issues and CO_2 emissions will progressively make a portion of the consumers switch to high-speed trains". The fool would scream: "Beware of the volcanic ash clouds!" We decided therefore to focus on identifying the 'real' experts, namely: people knowing consumers' needs (vendors, call center agents, cashiers), or people aware of new technologies (scientists, technicians).

An *innovation roadmap*—powerful framework often shared by marketing and R&D departments—will help you plan your projects.

In the upper part of the *innovation roadmap*, we identify new technologies, trends, new competitors and substitution products, as well as hazards likely to influence the target customers in the coming years. The timeline for analyzing these external factors may vary between 5 and 20 years depending on the industry. In the case of real estate, 20 years sounds good as the firm is also busy with designing and building the houses.

In the lower part of the *innovation roadmap*, we organize the internal innovation projects and product launches taking into account the external factors. Aligning our projects on external risks and opportunities will help increase the innovation hit rate.

Let us apply this tool to the high-speed trains case, with a focus on NS (Nederlandse Spoorwegen), the Dutch Railways. We can consider that horizon of 2020 is the right timeline.

For the Dutch Railways, external events occurring could be:

- *Flooding.* As the Netherlands is a country below the sea-level, flooding might be a threat for the Dutch infrastructure and NS should monitor the polar ice-cap meltdown.
- *Home-work.* Many Dutch people are already working from home 1 day a week. What if many of them work from home by 2015?
- *CO_2.* The regulations on CO_2 emissions are so far playing in favor of train travel. Major airlines have invested in the European high-speed train network.
- *Electric cars.* A new generation of electric cars, with a longer autonomy (thanks to an ingenious battery replacement system), could endanger trains and maybe even bikes.

Future Dutch Railways innovations could include (Fig. 5.13):

- *Training.* Increasing obesity could urge NS to set up a partnership with a fitness center and install training equipment on-board. This 'Train-ING' service would be sponsored by the ING bank.
- *MBA.* Why not study organizational behavior, corporate finance, and marketing strategy on the train? David Gardner, while proof-reading this chapter (thank you Dave, it was much needed!) shares that on the commuter train he occasionally rides from San Jose (Silicon Valley) to Stockton (Central Valley), in California, local universities started some "on-rail" training—the seminars held in one of the seating cars were "teasers" for full-scale classes and seminars. The power of *Wait Marketing* (Derval 2010) and innovation roadmaps.
- *Paris-Beijing.* HSR (High Speed Rail) offers great perspectives of expansion beyond European barriers. A Paris-Beijing line would boost the business with Middle-East and Asia.

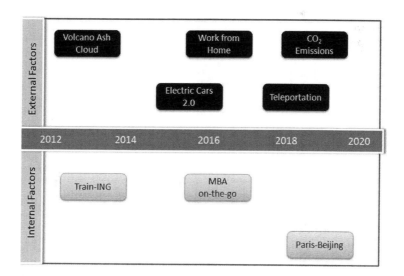

Fig. 5.13 Innovation roadmap of the Dutch Railways by 2020 (printed with DervalResearch permission)

China is building the largest high-speed train network. The Beijing-Shanghai line for instance has a length of 1,318 km and an expected travel speed of 350 km/h (Xinhua 2010). Given their growing economy, maybe they will buy parts of NS by 2017?

This rather crazy 'Paris-Beijing' train line—that started like a pure product of my retroduction—will happen for real, by 2025, and on the initiative of China! China plans to connect its train network with 17 countries by 2025, linking Asia with Europe (Moore 2010). This innovation roadmap does work.

When performing this "environmental scanning", it is important to identify the type of event, its source, its impact—positive or negative—its volatility, and the level of control the firm has on each risk (Department of the Premier and the Cabinet and Queensland Treasury 2007). It is also key to design an *innovation roadmap* per group of customers. If we think of our real estate case, we can foresee very different external factors (trends, substitution products) and internal projects for Bob and for Chris, justifying dedicated innovation roadmaps.

5.5.3 'Leadertips' to Winning Innovation

In a recent interview, the CEO of Berkshire Hathaway and the richest man of the US, Warren Buffet—with a fortune of $40 billion—shared his key to successful investment in eight rules (Money Programme Production 2009). He just invested in BYD, first electric car manufacturer in China, and demonstrated again the effectiveness of his approach to investment focusing on market trends and consumer needs. Let us see how these rules can help us innovate.

Rule #1: "*Invest, don't speculate*". If we consider innovation as a sustainable activity, we can look at the assets on the longer term, rather than being obsessed by stock price fluctuations. We can think of Häagen-Dazs in Chap. 3 supporting bees to save the vanilla.

Rule #2: "*You don't have to diversify*". The main idea is to innovate right rather than to develop a diverse portfolio. Björn Borg focusing on underwear, earlier in this chapter, is a good example.

Rule #3: "*Be a business owner*". The best way to understand markets and anticipate their developments is indeed to actively participate in the life of the products and services we develop. Meeting local clients, partners, and governmental representatives will help build a strong network and better anticipate risks and opportunities, as we will see in the Troon Golf success story later in this section.

Rule #4: "*Allocate capital efficiently*". When a feature is not important to the consumer, it is useless to invest R&D budget on it, even if it pleases the board or the development team, as demonstrated in the example of *Creative Labs* in Chap. 2.

Rule #5: "*Don't get into debt*". This advice can be interpreted as do not let others make important decisions impacting your innovations. Like *Red Bull* in Chap. 1, launching the cans in spite of the weird taste.

Rule #6: "*Think independently*". As an innovator, it is important to put in place a good information sources network. Having a quick conference call with business people and consumers would reveal more effective information in order to understand a sudden move than reading the press.

Rule #7: "*Break your own rules*". As an innovator, we must keep our freedom to make decisions and to adapt our process—it is the only way to improve and to stay versatile. If our tasting panel leads to wrong decisions like in Chap. 1 we should not hesitate to review the whole process.

Rule #8: "*Give it away*". Warren Buffet's motto is to re-distribute profits. Another way of sharing is to invest in innovation that positively changes people's life, like Velib' or Velodusche as shown in Chap. 2.

As a conclusion, there will always be great opportunities in the market for innovators who understand the underlying mechanisms and trends.

5.5.4 Hormonal Quotient^{TM} (HQ), Leadership, and Innovation

Current research confirms the influence of prenatal hormones on risk aversion (Roberti 2004).

The role of the board of directors and CEO in setting the firm's risk appetite and taste for innovation is key. So let us identify the persona of CEOs, measure their Hormonal Quotient^{TM} (HQ), analyze their leadership style, and share recommendations on how to align their innovation style with the firm's risk appetite (Derval 2010).

The highest level of risk is when a risk is not identified—in that matter the innovation map proposed earlier should greatly help—or worse, when the situation has been identified but ignored because its impact or probability were considered as negligible. A typical case is the IT project going wrong, mainly due to the project manager's overconfidence (Charette 2001). Often both the capacity of the firm to face the risk is overestimated and the seriousness of the risk is underestimated.

Not acknowledging that 'a risk is a risk' can happen even if a sophisticated strategic risks management framework is in place. The key actors in this 'taking a risk seriously' process are, as we will see later, the board of directors, and the CEO.

It seems that some leaders, like orange-blue tree lizards, do not perceive stress signals related to risks and therefore underestimate the likelihood of a product failure or its impact. We will see later that the Hormonal Quotient^{TM} (HQ) and leadership style of interviewed and measured leaders seem to confirm this hypothesis.

Let us have a closer look at 44 of my male students, leaders and managers enrolled in the Executive MBA program offered by the Robert Kennedy College in Zurich, affiliated to the University of Wales. We considered as top managers,

Table 5.5 Top managers by Hormonal Quotient™ (HQ)

		Top managers		Managers	Total	
	Very-testosterone	4	33.3%	2	6	13.6%
	Testosterone	1	8.3%	9	10	22.7%
	Balanced	2	16.7%	11	13	29.6%
	Estrogen	5	41.7%	10	15	34.1%
Total		12	100.0%	32	44	100.0%

Source: Research conducted by Prof. Diana Derval on 44 male participants in the program Robert Kennedy College, Executive MBA, enrolled in 2010

CEOs, general managers, VPs, and directors. Interestingly, top managers were over represented among very-testosterone and estrogen-driven students. For instance, estrogen-driven students represent 34.1% of the class and 41.7% of the top managers—one out of three estrogen-driven students is a top manager. Very-testosterone driven students represent only 13.6% of the class and 33.3% of the top managers—two out of three very-testosterone driven students are top managers. On the other hand, balanced students represent 29.6% of the class but only 16.7% of the top managers (Table 5.5).

Let us zoom into three of these successful leaders, with various Hormonal Quotient™ (HQ). We will add a feminine touch with the interview of the founder of *La Favorite*.

5.5.4.1 Estrogen-Driven—Innovator Type: "Collaborative Thinker"

Christopher, Hotel Manager of Sandals Resorts in St Lucia, is a Hotel and Resort professional. He has worked for Radisson, Hilton, Four Seasons, and Canadian Pacific (Fearmont Hotels) (Fig. 5.14).

Fig. 5.14 "Collaborative Thinker", estrogen-driven (printed with DervalResearch permission)

Fig. 5.15 "Networker", balanced (printed with DervalResearch permission

Leadership Style: "Process-Oriented". Christopher enjoys generating creative ideas together with his team: "I strongly believe that employees from various backgrounds, cultures and ages, if encouraged to 'think outside the box', will create an environment of innovation".

Very easy going and jovial, he describes his leadership as "firm, fair, and friendly". He leads in a very collaborative way, always taking his team's view into consideration, but does not negotiate with the rules.

Opportunities and Risks: Crisis. For the upcoming year, the American financial climate is a concern, as 75% of the market is from the US. The only way to attract customers was to lower the prices and propose a special "Luxury Included" deal. Christopher is clear: "The faster the economy recovers, the quicker we can get our pricing back to where it should be". This is the main opportunity to get some serious return on the millions of dollars invested during the recession "to upgrade our product offering for our customers".

Achievements: Customer Satisfaction. Since his tenure, 20% of the team had to be laid off. In spite of these limited resources, Christopher was able to increase the customers' satisfaction "to levels never before seen": "Two years ago I would never have dreamed that we would be in a position to better serve our customers with 20 percent less staff on the payroll. This has come about through strong leadership and motivation", he shares (Elliott 2010).

5.5.4.2 Balanced—Innovator Type: "Networker"

Saeed is the General Manager of Allegria Troon Golf Club in Cairo (Fig. 5.15).

Leadership Style: "Consultative". Due to the crisis, the golf industry has to find new reasons to attract and retain clients: "It is certain that focus on competitive golf activities alone does not deliver results. Instead we try to get people to try golf for fun and enjoy its social aspect."

In a manner similar to that of a hotel manager, he supervises sales and marketing, food and beverage, human resources, finance, housekeeping, administration, landscaping, but also golf operations and golf course maintenance. "A golf club has golfing services and social services—both are enjoyed by club members and guests", he adds.

Opportunities and Risks: Customers Attraction. The biggest opportunity is to attract new customer segments. The golf-course business requires huge investments: "Many golf courses are developed to be sold with a premiere golf course view and with a long-term future in mind." The owners of the course are SODIC, and Troon Golf, world leader in golf course management, development, and marketing.

Achievements: Stakeholders' Satisfaction. "I take pride and fulfillment in mentoring, training, and developing associates and managers", says Saeed. Investors' satisfaction is also his concern and he makes sure to maintain a "sustainable market position along with good financial returns." Allegria was named Best Development and Best Golf Course by CNBC Property Awards in 2008 (Elgazar 2010).

5.5.4.3 Very-Testosterone—Innovator Type: "Dominator"

Derek is CEO at Tawasul Telecoms in Kuwait. He was appointed 9 months ago to relaunch the company (Fig. 5.16).

Leadership Style: "Performer". Derek is observing competitors in order to secure the newly market leader role of Tawasul Telecoms: "Our positioning of dominant player pays tribute to our adopted Blue Ocean approach." He adds that the former biggest competitor is "now reselling our products and services to our other partners". After a period of observation, he found out "what was wrong with this picture": "Many of the senior managers had built pyramids of power, and as they didn't posses the correct knowledge for the telecommunications wholesale industry, this led the company to under perform and chase 'castles in the sky'". Once he had replaced this part of the staff, Derek was able to go back to a more

Fig. 5.16 "Dominator", very testosterone-driven (printed with DervalResearch permission)

participative style "pulling instead of pushing". He manages five senior teams, and 125 people across four countries in the Gulf.

Opportunities and Risks: Expansion. The main challenges are to maintain the current level of innovation and attract top senior managers with more 'Thought Leadership' skills. Derek sees Europe as a target, in order to get close to the firm's partners: "We should look at expansion through acquisition, if this is not supported by the board we will be limited like a 'bird in a golden cage'—this will mean a stagnation in growth, which will result in our need to enter home-grown markets (products and services) where the margins are very low but the volumes are high."

Achievements: "Uber-Achieving". Derek is proud of Tawasul results: the sales doubled, the objectives are "over-achieved by 15%". He was also able to "implement a true 'team geist' across the board and at all levels, fostering innovation, being the doctor that healed the corporate identity, and attracting 5 tier 1 operators into announcing Tawasul as their preferred partner in the region" (Hellmons 2010).

5.5.4.4 Testosterone-Driven—Innovator Type: "Creator"

Brigit, founder of La Favorite—we studied the success story of her divan for Very Important Pets in Chap. 4—illustrates well a testosterone-driven leader. A former trader with a flair for luxury and design, she took a mini-MBA class for women entrepreneurs at ESSEC Paris–Singapore Business School to turn her vision into a winning brand.

Leadership Style: "Result-Oriented". Visionary entrepreneur, she keeps herself busy anticipating customers needs in her industry. Always sourcing new natural and recycled materials: "Our perfect understanding of the context demonstrates *La Favorite's* know-how". Innovation comes also from an exclusive positioning, opening new opportunities (Fig. 5.17).

Brigit Mettra, ex-trader, is result-oriented. She listens to others, takes advice, and sometimes changes her mind. She insists "I make the final decision on my own". She is very demanding and never loses the focus on the set objectives. As *La Favorite* is a young company, so far she manages mainly designers, partners, and manufacturers.

Fig. 5.17 "Creator", testosterone-driven (printed with DervalResearch permission)

Opportunities and Risks: International Expansion. Brigit considers there is always a risk in business. A strategic risk for the brand this year would be not being able to implement the needed international expansion—as opportunities are increasingly coming from the US and from Asia.

Achievements: R&D. Brigit is very proud of having created a brand from A to Z with a masterpiece, the Sofa O', that required 8 months of R&D because of strong design constraints. "Of course our first sale with the luxury Parisian hotel *Le Meurice* was a high point in the firm's development," she adds.

Interestingly, our testosterone-driven leaders—Derek, and Brigit—are into creating markets, expanding internationally, being the clear deciders, putting their ideas into motion, working in technological environments, involving R&D. The extra testosterone seems to lead indeed to some "male:male" competition and to trigger the willingness not only to create but to lead people towards uncontestable success.

On the other hand, our estrogen-driven leaders—Saeed, and Christopher—are into attracting and retaining more clients in their market, building strong relationships with all stakeholders, involving their teams and generating ideas together, optimizing processes in a crisis-context. The extra estrogen seems to encourage co-idea generation.

Once their own Hormonal Quotient™ (HQ) has been identified, the innovation roadmap is designed, the strategic objectives, risk appetite and tolerance are set, the board of directors or CEO can appoint a leader with an innovation profile aligned with:

- *The strategy.* If the firm needs short term Blue Ocean strategies, a testosterone-driven innovator, men or women, will be perfect.
- *The participation level of the Board.* If the Board wants to co-decide, an estrogen-driven innovator, man or woman, will be the perfect pick.
- *The partners' way of doing business.* If the firm plans to develop external informal networking in China, then an estrogen-driven leader might be the smart choice, as they will be more naturally diplomatic.

Alternatively, the board can name an innovation champion to counterbalance the bias of the leader, whether he/she does not perceive risk or does not perceive them as stressful. The champion would increase risk management awareness, and help assess risks in coordination with the board and the CEO (Department of the Premier and the Cabinet and Queensland Treasury 2007).

From lizards to leaders, the role of prenatal hormones is considerable in driving people towards entrepreneur or innovator's vocations, in shaping their leadership style, influencing the industry they work in, their team management style, their willingness to expand, to create, to share, as well as their decision process (Derval 2010).

Boards of directors and CEOs can use the Hormonal Quotient™ (HQ) to better understand, predict, and manage the strategic risk, linked to the development of new products and services.

And you, what type of innovator are you? You can evaluate your Hormonal Quotient[TM] (HQ) at www.derval-research.com.

5.6 Take-Aways

Market Prospective

- For any unexpected event occurring, there is someone who knew.
- Identifying and interviewing the right experts is critical.
- Observing market trends for each type of consumer separately helps.

Vision

- 25% of the people, super-beamers, are very sensitive to light.
- Short wavelength colors, like blue, relax nearsighted individuals.
- Women with very-testosterone and estrogen Hormonal Quotient[TM] (HQ) prefer violet.

Neurosciences

- Statistics have little to do with science.
- Mapping the brain, and counting genes, can be as useless as making a survey.
- Understanding 'why' is more important than locating 'where'.

Planning Success

- Once we can predict consumers' behavior, it is possible to plan success.
- The leader's Hormonal Quotient[TM] (HQ) defines the firm's innovation roadmap.
- Form your own opinion based on analogy.

References

Alexander G (2003) An evolutionary perspective of sex-typed toy preferences: pink, blue, and the brain. Sex Behav 32(1):7–14

Bar M (2007) The proactive brain: using analogies and associations to generate predictions. Trends Cognitive Sci 11:280–289

Baraas R, Carroll J, Gunther K, Chung M, Williams D, Foster D et al (2007) Adaptive optics retinal imaging reveals S-cone dystrophy in tritan color-vision deficiency. J Opt Soc America 23(5):1438–1447

Brennicke R (2010, January 16) Marketing Director, Björn Borg (D. Derval, Interviewer)

Calkins D (2001) Seeing with S cones. Prog Retin Eye Res 20:255–287

Carl Zeiss Vision (2010) Eye and vision. From Carl Zeiss vision. http://www.vision.zeiss.com/C1256FBA0032FCC7/Contents-Frame/CF8FBDA83BE0A848C125720B00521D8C. Accessed May 2010

Chan S (2010, March 16) Mix10: the Bing blue color that's worth $80 million. From The Seattle Times. http://seattletimes.nwsource.com/html/microsoftpri0/2011361493_mix10_the_bing_blue_color_thats_worth_80_million.html. Accessed 5 May 2010

Charette R (2001) The risks with risk identification. From ITHABI Corporation. http://www. itmpi.org/assets/base/images/itmpi/privaterooms/robertcharette/RISK_ID.pdf. Accessed 10 May 2010

Cho N, Poulsen G, Ver Hoeve J, Nork T (2000) Selective loss of S-cones in diabetic retinopathy. Arch Opthalmol 118:1393–1400

Colman D (2009, October 30) Greenspan's underpants. From New York Magazine. http://nymag.com/news/intelligencer/61748/. Accessed 10 May 2010

Department of the Premier and Cabinet, Queensland Treasury (2007) Strategic risk management: guidelines. Department of the Premier and Cabinet, Queensland Treasury

Derval D (2009) Wait Marketing: is it the right moment? DervalResearch, Amsterdam

Derval D (2010) Lizards and hazards: The impact of hormones on leadership style, and strategic risk management. ISM, Paris

Eisner A, Fleming S, Kleins M, Mauldin W (1987) Sensitivities in older eyes with good acuity: cross-sectional norms. Invest Ophthalmol Vis Sci 28(11):1824–1831

Elgazar S (2010, April 6) General Manager at Troon Golf in Egypt (D. Derval, Interviewer)

Elliott C (2010, April 6) Hotel Manager Sandal Resorts in St Lucia (D. Derval, Interviewer)

Epilepsy Foundation (2010) Seizures and syndromes. From Epilepsy Foundation. http://www.epilepsyfoundation.org/about/types/index.cfm. Accessed 5 May 2010

Fuller R, Fleishman L, Leal M, Travis J, Loew E (2004) Intraspecific variation in retinal cone distribution in the bluefin killifish, lucania foodei. J Comp Physiol A: Neuroethol Sens Neural Behav Physiol 189(8):609–616

Gerardin P (2005) Configural and perceptual factors influencing the perception of color transparency. Universite Lumiere, Lyon

Goodwyn W (2007, October 24) In Dallas, a Hip-Hop Plea: pull your pants up. From National Public Radio.http://www.npr.org/templates/story/story.php?storyId=15534306. Accessed 10 May 2010

Haier R, Karama S, Leyba L, Jung R (2009) MRI assessment of cortical thickness and functional activity changes in adolescent girls following three months of practice on a visual-spatial task. BMC Res Notes 2:174

Hedge A (2010) Visual performance course. Cornell University, New York

Hellmons D (2010, April 6) CEO of Tawasul Telecoms (D. Derval, Interviewer)

Hussey ES (2003) Speculations on the nature of visual motion optometric implications. Retrieved from The Journal of Behavioral Optometry.http://www.oepf.org/jbo/journals/14-5%20 Hussey.pdf

Jaseja H (2008) Scientific basis behind traditional practice of application of "shoe-smell" in controlling epileptic seizures in the eastern countries. Clin Neurol Neurosurg 110(6):535–538

Kimberly J, Highnote S, Wasserman L (2001) Richer color experience in observers with multiple photopigment opsin genes. Psychon Soc 8(2):244–261

Kraus J (2005) The ABCs of SETI: the search for extraterrestrial intelligence. From Big Ear Radio Observatory.http://www.bigear.org/seti.htm. Accessed 10 May 2010

Krug H (2010, January 12) Director Corporate R&D, Carl Zeiss Vision (D. Derval, Interviewer)

Kudo H, Dunbar R (2001) Neocortex size and social network size in primates. Anim Behav 62(4):711–722

Langer N, Beeli B, Jancke L (2010) When the sun prickles your nose: an EEG study identifying neural bases of photic sneezing. PLoS ONE 5(2):e9208

Liang K, Hon W, Tyan Y, Liao W (1994) Involvement of hippocampal NMDA and AMPA receptors in acquisition, formation and retrieval of spatial memory in the Morris water maze. Chin J Physiol 37(4):201–212

Maguire E, Gadian D, Johnsrude I, Good C, Ashburner J, Frackowiak R et al (2000) Navigation-related structural change in the hippocampi of taxi drivers. Proc Natl Acad Sci USA 97(8):4398–4403

Marieb EN (2007) The special senses. In: Marieb EN (ed) Human anatomy and physiology, 7th edn. Pearson Education, San Francisco, pp 555–603

Hines M, Fane B, Pasterski V, Mathews G (2003) Spatial abilities following prenatal androgen abnormality: targeting and mental rotations performance in individuals with congenital adrenal hyperplasia. Psychoneuroendocrinology 28(8):1010–1026

McMahon C, Carroll J, Awua S, Neitz J, Neitz M (2008) The L:M cone ratio in males of African descent with normal color vision. J Vis 232(4747):193–202

Money Programme Production (2009) Warren Buffet (Director), How to be Rich [Motion Picture]

Moore M (2010, March 8) King's Cross to Beijing in two days on new high-speed rail network. Telegraph.co.uk. http://www.telegraph.co.uk/news/worldnews/asia/china/7397846/Kings-Cross-to-Beijing-in-two-days-on-new-high-speed-rail-network.html. Accessed 10 April 2010

Nakano T, Yamamoto Y, Kitajo K, Takahashi T, Kitazawa S (2009) Synchronization of spontaneous eyeblinks while viewing video stories. Proc R Soc B 276(1673):3635–3644

Neitz J, Carroll J, Neitz M (2001, January) Color vision: almost reason enough for having eyes. Optics Photonics News 2(1):26–33

NeuroProbes (2010) Home. From Neuroprobes. http://naranja.umh.es/~np/. Accessed 10 May 2010

Pardo P, Perez A, Suero M (2007) An example of sex-linked color vision differences. Color Res Appl 32(6):433–439

Pinel JP (2007) Basics of biopsychology. Pearson Education, Boston

Roberti JW (2004) A review of behavioral and biological correlates of sensation seeking. J Res Pers 38(3):256–279

sharp-sighted.org (2009) Intro. Retrieved from Sharp-Sighted.org-facial masking, alignment and dyslexia. http://www.sharp-sighted.org

Stockman A, Brainard DH (2009) Color vision mechanisms. Retrieved from color & vision research laboratory and database. http://cvision.ucsd.edu/people/Stockman/pubs/2009%20Color%20Vision%20Mechanisms%20SB.pdf

Trackmania (2010) Trackmania home page. From Trackmania:http://www.trackmania.com/. Accessed 5 May 2010

US 1/212th Aviation Regiment Flight Training Guide (2003) Night Study Guide, US Army

Vallortigara G, Rogers L (2005) Survival with an asymmetrical brain: advantages and disadvantages of cerebral lateralization. Behav Brain Sci 28(4):575–589

Vitale S, Sperduto R, Ferris F (2009) Increased prevalence of myopia in the United States between 1971–1972 and 1999 and 2004. Arch Ophthalmol 127:1632–1639

Xinhua (2010, March 4) China building World's largest high speed rail network. From china daily. http://www.chinadaily.com.cn/china/2010-03/04/content_9538323.htm. Accessed 5 April 2010

About the Author

Diana Derval is President and Research Director of DervalResearch, a global market research firm specializing in human perception and behavior, and Chair of the Board of Directors of the Better Immune System Foundation.

Visionary researcher, inventor of the Hormonal Quotient™ (HQ), member of the Society for Behavioral Neuroendocrinology, and author regularly featured in the media, Diana Derval turns fascinating neuroscientific breakthroughs into powerful business frameworks to identify, understand, and predict human traits, motivations, and behavior. She has accelerated the development of Fortune 500 firms including TomTom, Michelin, HP, Philips, Sara Lee, and Danone.

Diana Derval is Adjunct Professor of Marketing and Innovation at the Robert Kennedy College, and teaches Sensory Science at ESSEC Paris-Singapore Business School and at the University Leonard de Vinci. Over 10,000 professionals have enjoyed her inspirational lectures and workshops from Chicago to Shanghai.

Diana Derval has decided to donate all her royalties on the sales of this book to the Better Immune System Foundation, to encourage research, prevention, and information programs.

About DervalResearch

DervalResearch is the worldwide leading research firm in behavioral neuroendocrinology applied to product development. With powerful predictive models like the Hormonal Quotient™ (HQ), their team of scientists helps firms increase their innovation hit rate and deliver the right sensory mix.

You will find more information at http://www.derval-research.com.

About Better Immune System

Many immune system disorders like eczema, asthma, sinusitis, hyperacusis, diabetes, autism, and more are in fact related to our hormonal balance. The mission of the Foundation is to conduct research, information and prevention programs for a Better Immune System. As an Individual or a Corporation, you can select the programs you wish to support at http://www.betterimmunesystem.org.

We thank you for your contribution.

Conclusion

While writing this book, I discovered I was slightly autistic, testosterone-driven, super-taster, photic sneezer with a wide M-pathway, not colorblind, allergic to synthetic fragrances, and a 'creator' type of innovator.

I hope you also learned a lot about your customers and yourself during this journey.

Just being aware of the fact that individuals have a different sensory perception, that this perception is linked to hormones, and that we can therefore predict consumers' preferences and behavior is a gigantic competitive advantage for your company.

I hope that each chapter gave you more knowledge, tools, and method, in order to apply this approach to your business and market. I will be happy to hear your feedback and questions at diana.derval@derval-research.com or on the Facebook page http://www.facebook.com/pages/The-Right-Sensory-Mix/123804197658095. At DervalResearch's website http://www.derval-research.com, you will find online tests and experiments linked to taste, hearing, vision, smell, touch, and more.

I have decided to donate my royalties to the Better Immune System Foundation http://www.betterimmunesystem.org to encourage research on disorders linked with sensory perception. Your direct support is of course much appreciated.

Cordialement

Diana Derval

Index